America's
Coming
Crisis

*prophetic warnings,
divine destiny*

America's
Coming
Crisis

prophetic warnings,
divine destiny

David N. Balmforth

First Printing: October 1998

International Standard Book Number:
0-88290-631-3

Horizon Publishers' Catalog and Order Number:
1088

Printed and distributed
in the United States of America by

Horizon
Publishers
& Distributors, Incorporated

Mailing Address:
P.O. Box 490
Bountiful, Utah 84011-0490

Street Address:
50 South 500 West
Bountiful, Utah 84010

Local Phone: (801) 295-9451
WATS (toll free): 1 (800) 453-0812
FAX: (801) 295-0196

Internet: www.horizonpublishers.com

Contents

Dedication

To my family and friends who inspired in me a great love of this country and an understanding of her divine mission to the world.

To those of you who will be ready to step forth at some future period of time to rescue and redeem those sacred principles of liberty upon which our great American republic was founded.

I know these are unpleasant things. It is not a pleasant thing even for me to stand here and tell you that this is written in the Scriptures. If the Lord has a controversy with the nations, He will put them to the sword. Their bodies shall lie unburied like dung upon the earth. That is not nice, is it, but should we not know it? Is it not our duty to read these things and understand them? Don't you think the Lord has given us these things that we might know and we might prepare ourselves through humility, through repentance, through faith, that we might escape from these dreadful conditions that are portrayed by these ancient prophets? That is why I am reading them. I feel just as keenly as you do about the condition, and I pray for it to come to an end, but I want it to come to an end right.[1]

—Joseph Fielding Smith

---

[1] Joseph Fielding Smith, *Signs of the Times*, pp. 154-155.

Foreword

I believe the Constitution of this great country was framed under the inspiration and blessings of God. I further believe that it is the greatest document of human liberty that has ever been conceived by the mind of man. A document made up of eternal and "holy principles" (D&C 101:77) and established "by the hands of wise men" (D&C:101:80) whom the Lord held in reserve to come forth in his own due time, proudly waving the banner of liberty and equal rights to all the world and to all men.

America has passed through and overcome many dangers since her founding in 1776. I believe she is now entering the gravest and most dangerous period of her existence. The infiltration of immoral ideologies and practices that are destructive to our God-given freedoms have made serious inroads, thus weakening these divine Constitutional principles of human liberty. Her spiritual and moral foundations are being attacked and dismantled from within at an alarming rate. Lawlessness and gang warfare are increasing throughout the nation, while permissiveness and moral decay are becoming the norm.

In 1831, as a French visitor to this country, Alexis de Tocqueville made a detailed study of the reasons for the incredible success of our country and what made her great. He later gave this thoughtful analysis of what would happen if America ever ceased to be a moral and righteous country and departed from the principles that led to her preeminence in the world:

> I sought for the greatness and genius of America in her commodious harbors and her ample rivers, and it was not there; in her fertile fields and boundless prairies, and it was not there; in her rich mines and her vast

world commerce, and it was not there. Not until I went to the churches of America and heard her pulpits aflame with righteousness did I understand the secret of her genius and power. *America is great because she is good, and if America ever ceases to be good, she will cease to be great.* (emphasis added)[1]

The dangers de Tocqueville warned of were what Nephi foresaw happening in the "last days." Nephi saw that the inhabitants of this great gentile nation would indeed become so proud, wicked and "drunken with iniquity and all manner of abominations" (2 Ne. 27:1), that they would be destroyed by the hand of the Lord. He saw that this great destruction would come upon them because of their "murders, and robbing, and lying, and deceivings, and whoredoms, and all manner of abominations." (Mormon 8:31) In addition, Nephi saw that the Lord would visit the "perverse and stiffnecked" (Mormon 8:33) inhabitants of this land "with sore affliction, with pestilence, with plague, with sword" (D&C 97:26) and with earthquake, storm, tempest, and "the flame of devouring fire." (2 Ne. 27:2)

This is a choice land, a land especially designated of God, and He has placed an "everlasting decree" upon all those whom He allows to possess it that they shall serve Him or they "shall be swept off . . . And it is not until the fulness of iniquity among the children of the land, that they are swept off. (Ether 2:8-10)."

We will discuss just how these future events may happen, how they might relate to and could be brought about by any of the current flash-point crises in the world today. There are numerous other recommended books that are keystone to this future period of time such as: *Prophecy—Key to the Future* and *Inspired Prophetic Warnings* by Duane S. Crowther, and *Prophecy and Modern Times* by W. Cleon Skousen, as well as others, which have added to our

---

[1] As quoted by Ezra Taft Benson in, *God, Family, Country: Our Three Great Loyalties*, p. 360.

knowledge of the future destiny of America and her inhabitants.

In this book we will review the blessings that God is willing to bestow upon America if she will but serve him, the historic parallels between those ancient civilizations that once possessed this land prior to their demise and our own, and how wickedness, corruption and the setting up of secret combinations may bring about a similar fate and annihilation to America. We will explain how this future period of great destruction and tribulation may come about through the unleashing of atomic, biological and chemical weapons of war, what the Saints can do to prepare and what the final destiny of America, as a nation, and of the earth shall be.

—David N. Balmforth

A Christian Nation Is Born

The United States of America has, in a very short period of time, become one of the greatest and most prosperous nations which has ever existed. This has come about largely because of the Christian principles of liberty that she has come to symbolize and embody to all the world. She has become known in both song and lore as the "land of the free and the home of the brave." We are a nation of immigrants dedicated to the perpetuation of individual liberties and the inalienable rights of man. In the following pages we will not only examine the role that the Lord has had in the founding and growth of this great constitutional republic, but also what awaits this nation if we ever completely turn from these noble principles.

America, Land with a Divine Destiny

Latter-day Saints should strive to make themselves familiar with the foreordination and destiny of the American nation because of the great influence, power and pre-eminence the Lord tells us she is to achieve in the world. The Savior tells us that these blessings of freedom and liberty have come about through the "wisdom" and "the power of the Father" (3 Ne. 21:4).

We should also study and be aware of the reasons for the destruction and demise of the great ancient civilizations that once flourished here on the American continent, comparing what happened to them with the visions of the future-prophesied destruction and cleansing of the United States of America and its people.

In First Nephi we learn that "the Lord hath created the earth that it should be inhabited; and he hath created his

children that they should possess it" and also that "he
leadeth away the righteous into *precious lands*, and the
wicked he destroyeth, and curseth the land unto them for
their sakes" (1 Ne. 17:36, 38; emphasis added). The Lord
has blessed America by "decree" to become the most prosperous and bountiful country in the world. It is a "choice"
land *"above all other lands"* (Ether 2:9-10; emphasis
added). It has an abundance of fertile land, forests, precious minerals and wild life.

America Hidden by the Hand of the Lord

In Second Nephi the Lord explains his involvement and
guidance of events in the Americas when He explains that
"it is wisdom that this land should be kept as yet from the
knowledge of other nations; for behold, many nations
would overrun the land, that there would be no place for
an inheritance (2 Ne. 1:8)." After explaining the reason He
has kept this land hidden from the knowledge of other
nations we can understand more clearly why He has
emphatically stated

> . . . that there shall none come unto this land, save they
> shall be brought by the hand of the Lord.
> Wherefore, this land is consecrated unto him whom he
> shall bring. And if it so be that they shall serve him accord-
> ing to the commandments which he hath given, it shall be
> a land of liberty unto them; wherefore, they shall never be
> brought down into captivity; if so, it shall be because of
> iniquity; for if iniquity shall abound, cursed shall be the
> land for their sakes; but unto the righteous it shall be
> blessed for ever (2 Ne. 1:6-7).

Led by the Spirit,
Columbus Rediscovers the Americas

In 1492, the Spirit of the Lord influenced, inspired and
motivated a daring mariner, Christopher Columbus, to
brave the hidden passageway across the great deep and
rediscover this land of promise.

Nephi, in vision, described the descent and inspiration of the Holy Ghost upon Columbus: "And I looked and beheld a man among the Gentiles, who was separated from the seed of my brethren by the many waters; and I beheld the Spirit of God, that it came down and wrought upon the man; and he went forth upon the many waters, even unto the seed of my brethren, who were in the promised land." (1 Ne. 13:12) "*The man referred to in this scripture was Columbus*," declared President Hinckley,[1] then first counselor in the First Presidency, as he spoke at a fireside at the Bountiful/Woods Cross Regional Center, on July 19, 1992. Columbus himself acknowledged the influence the Spirit of the Lord had upon him as the following excerpts from his personal writings illustrate:

> With a hand that could be felt, the Lord opened my mind to the fact that it would be possible to sail from here to the Indies. . . . This was a fire that burned within me . . . who can doubt that this fire was not merely mine, but also of the Holy Spirit.[2]

> From my first youth onward, I was a seaman and have so continued until this day. . . . Wherever on the earth a ship has been, I have been. I have spoken and treated with learned men, priests, and laymen, Latins, and Greeks, Jews and Moors, and with many men of other faiths. The Lord was well disposed to my desire, and He bestowed upon me courage and understanding; knowledge of seafaring.

> He gave me in abundance, of astrology as much as was needed, and of geometry and astronomy likewise.

> Further, He gave me joy and cunning in drawing maps and thereon cities, mountains, rivers, islands, and harbours, each one in its place. I have seen and truly I have studied all books—cosmographies, histories, chronicles,

---

[1] "Columbus, Pioneers 'Courageous,'" *Church News*, July 25, 1992.

[2] Arnold K. Garr, *Christopher Columbus: A Latter-day Saint Perspective*, p. 41.

and philosophies, and other arts, for which our Lord unlocked my mind, sent me upon the sea, and gave me fire for the deed. Those who heard of my enterprise called it foolish, mocked me, and laughed. *But who can doubt but that the Holy Ghost inspired me?*[3]

An article in the *Church News* in 1992, celebrating the 500th anniversary of Columbus and his divine voyage of discovery to America, had this to say:

Columbus' history-making journey to America opened the door to a flood of exploration, colonization, missionary work and fortune-seeking. But more important, it was fulfillment of prophecy uttered more than 2,000 years earlier and established Columbus as a forerunner to the restoration of the gospel.

. . . Historians are not at a loss for references by Columbus which boldly declare that the Lord directed him in his great undertaking. His journals and other personal writings are replete with such statements. Referring to his first voyage to America, he once stated:

"Who can doubt that this fire was not merely mine, but also of the Holy Spirit who encouraged me with the radiance of marvelous illumination from his sacred Holy Scriptures, by a most clear and powerful testimony . . . urging me to press forward? Continually, without a moments hesitation, the Scriptures urged me to press forward with great haste." (*El Libro de las Profecias de Christopher Columbus*, p. 105.)

In *The Geographical Conceptions of Columbus*, (p. 43), George E. Nunn asserts that Columbus "*did not make a single false move the entire voyage.*" (emphasis added)

. . . Nunn suggests that Columbus' success was the result of "an application of reason to knowledge." Columbus, however, gives credit to the Lord. Even though he was a successful seaman and an accomplished navigator, he said, "Our Lord opened to my understanding. (I could

---

[3] Jacob Wassermann, *Columbus, Don Quixote of the Seas,* translated by Eric Sutton, pp. 19-20 (emphasis added).

sense His hand upon me), so that it became clear to me that it was feasible to navigate from here to the Indies. (Christopher Columbus' Book of Prophecies, p. 178.) Columbus always referred to America as the Indies.

. . . Morison, in his Pulitzer Prize-winning biography of Columbus declares, "there can be no doubt that the faith of Columbus was genuine and sincere, and that his frequent communion with forces unseen was a vital element in his achievement." (*Admiral of the Open Sea*, p. 65.)

Columbus not only believed that the Lord inspired him on his first voyage, but was also convinced that the Holy Scriptures prophesied of his great enterprise. During the last years of his life, he was working on a manuscript that he never finished, entitled Book of Prophecies. This work includes a collection of prophetic passages, especially from the Book of Isaiah, which he believed pertained to his expedition.[4]

Columbus also felt that he had a divine calling to be an emissary of the Lord to spread the tenets of Christianity throughout the world:

I feel persuaded, by the many and wonderful manifestations of Divine Providence in my especial favour, that I am the chosen instrument of God in bringing to pass a great event—no less than the conversion of millions who are now existing in the darkness of Paganism.[5]

Columbus remained true to his belief that the Lord and the Holy Spirit had been his constant companion throughout his life, and upon his deathbed in the year 1506 he uttered his final words, "*Into your hands, O Lord, I commend my spirit.*"[6] His journey was finished, his earthly mission accomplished and he returned home to his trusted Father.

---

[4] "1492 Voyage Fulfilled Prophecy," *Church News*, Vol. 62, No. 39, September 26, 1992, pp. 7, 10 (emphasis added).
[5] Arnold K. Garr, *Christopher Columbus*, Appendix B, p. 82.
[6] *Op. Cit.*

Many of our church leaders such as Brigham Young,[7] Wilford Woodruff,[8] George Q. Cannon,[9] Orson Hyde,[10] Mark E. Petersen,[11] Spencer W. Kimball,[12] and Ezra Taft Benson[13] have testified of the divine guidance given Columbus and his inspired role in the rediscovery of the American continent.

In summarizing the life of Columbus it has been said that there were several spiritual aspects of it that affected the Americas:

(1) His discovery of the New World for Europe fulfilled Book of Mormon prophecy. (2) He served as a forerunner to the Restoration. (3) The primary motivation for his exploration was not financial gain, but the spread of Christianity. (4) He was guided by the Spirit of God, most especially on his first voyage to the Americas. (5) He himself believed that he was guided by the Spirit. (6) He regarded many of his achievements as a fulfillment of biblical and other prophecy.[14]

Early church leader and apostle, George Q. Cannon, made this statement relating to the preparatory calling and mission of Columbus:

Columbus was inspired to penetrate the ocean and discover this Western continent, for the set time for its discovery had come, and the consequences which God desired to follow its discovery have taken place—a free government has been established on it. The men who established that Government were inspired of God—George

---

[7] See Brigham Young, *Journal of Discourses*, Vol. 7, p. 13.

[8] See Wilford Woodruff, *Journal of Discourses*, Vol. 23, p. 81.

[9] See George Q. Cannon, *Journal of Discourses*, Vol. 14, p. 55; Vol. 19, p. 202; Vol. 23, p. 102.

[10] See Orson Hyde, *Journal of Discourses*, Vol. 6, p. 368.

[11] See Mark E. Petersen, *The Great Prologue*, pp. 2-3.

[12] See Edward L. Kimball, Editor, *The Teachings of Spencer W. Kimball*, p. 427.

[13] See Ezra Taft Benson, *The Teachings of Ezra Taft Benson*, p. 577.

[14] FARMS, *Review of Books*, Vol. 8, No. 1, p. 111.

Washington, Thomas Jefferson, John Adams, Benjamin Franklin, and all the fathers of the Republic were inspired to do the work which they did. We believe it was a preparatory work for the establishment of the kingdom of God. This Church and kingdom could not have been established on the earth if their work had not been performed.[15]

As Mark E. Petersen so aptly pointed out: "Thus we see that it was the Lord's will that only those settlers came to America to make permanent homes who were so permitted by the Lord Himself, people who would fit his program for the restoration of the gospel."[16]

Jamestown Colonized

In 1607 the hand of the Lord guided another attempt to colonize this great consecrated land of America at a place called Jamestown. It was to become the first permanent North American colony of England. It began in the American wilderness of what became known as the state of Virginia.

W. Cleon Skousen explains the significance and difference this particular colonization effort had upon generations of mankind:

> The most striking thing about the settlers of Jamestown was their startling similarity to the ancient pioneers who built settlements in other parts of the world 5,000 years earlier. The whole panorama of Jamestown demonstrated how shockingly, little progress had been made by man during all of those fifty centuries.
>
> The settlers of Jamestown had come in a boat no larger and no more commodious than those of the ancient sea kings. Their tools still consisted of shovel, axe, hoe, and a stick plow which were only slightly improved over those of China, Egypt, Persia, and Greece. They harvested their grain and hay-grass with the same primitive scythes. They wore clothes made of thread spun on a wheel and woven

---

[15] George Q. Cannon, *Journal of Discourses*, Vol. 14, p. 55.
[16] Mark E. Petersen, *The Great Prologue*, p. 31.

by hand. They thought alcohol was a staple food. Their medicines were noxious concoctions based on superstition rather than science. Their transportation was by cart and oxen.

Most of them died young. Out of approximately 9,000 settlers who found their way to old Jamestown, only about 1,000 survived.

But potentially, Jamestown was different.

. . . Eventually, it was in Jamestown that a system of free enterprise principles began to filter up through the years of "Starving time" to impress on the settlers those dynamic ideas which were later refined and developed in Adam Smith's famous book, *The Wealth of Nations*.

. . . The descendants of these Virginia settlers produced many of the foremost intellects who structured the framework for the new civilization which became known as the United States of America. From among them came Thomas Jefferson, author of the Declaration of Independence; James Madison, "father" of the Constitution; George Washington, hero general of the War for Independence; George Mason, author of the first American Bill of Rights in Virginia . . . and she furnished four of the first five Presidents of the United States.

. . . The spirit of freedom which moved out across the world in the 1800s was primarily inspired by the fruits of freedom in the United States.[17]

The Pilgrims Arrive Aboard the Mayflower

In 1620 the hand of the Lord brought another important nonconformist group of immigrants to America aboard the Mayflower. They were members of the Puritan and Separatist movement in England and they were seeking refuge from the religious tyranny and oppression experienced under the Church of England. These colonists founded the second permanent settlement in America and became known as the *Pilgrims*.

---

[17] W. Cleon Skousen, *The Five Thousand Year Leap*, pp. 1-3.

After a momentous and exhausting voyage across the ocean, as their ship lay anchored off Cape Cod Harbor, William Bradford states that they were faced with "some discontents and murmurings . . . amongst some, and mutinous speeches and carriages in other[s]." This potential insurrection and anarchy from among some of their group was "soon quelled and overcome by the wisdom and patience" of the wiser ones among them.[18] On November 21, 1620 (then November 11) this crisis caused them to gather together in the cabin aboard the ship and gave birth to the formation of the first agreement for self-government ever put in force in America, the Mayflower Compact. It was this group of courageous wanderers that brought forth that famous document that has inspired and influenced our republican form of government more than any other with the possible exception of the Magna Charta. In the April, 1960 General Conference, Levi Edgar Young stressed to the Saints the importance of these Pilgrims on the founding of this nation and our way of life:

> It was by divine guidance that the Pilgrim Fathers came to America and planted here the institutions of civilization. By the Mayflower Compact they established a republic, the highest form of political institution known to man. Such a republic was unknown up to their time, and this was the only land where a nation of this kind was possible. This continent had been unknown until right men, rightly trained, could build their homes in the wilderness and hold the ground for a purpose larger than they knew. These Christians had in mind a new city of God in the wilderness, and they made the fish the emblem of their commonwealth, which has from old been the symbol of Christian humility.[19]

---

[18] William Bradford, *History of Plymouth Plantation 1620-1647*, Vol. 1, pp. 192-193.

[19] Levi Edgar Young, *Conference Report*, April, 1960, p. 63.

This nation's history is firmly established with a reliance on a Supreme Being that has been recognized in many of its historical documents such as the Mayflower Compact, Declaration of Independence, Lincoln's Gettysburg Address, the National Anthem, "In God We Trust" on our currency and the words "under God" in our Pledge of Allegiance. Kenneth D. Wells, in an address given at BYU, explained how the founders were well taught in the history of the nations that came before them and recognized God's influence upon man's search for freedom:

> When the Declaration of Independence was written, our wise forefathers were schooled in the history of man's quest for freedom. They had the Magna Charta of 1215 clearly in mind. They understood it. There are supposed to be nine men who signed that Declaration who knew the Magna Charta by heart. Others knew the soul-stirring words in the leading sentence of the Mayflower Compact: "In the name of God, Amen." They knew of the Petition of Right of 1628, and they knew of the Federal Orders of Connecticut of 1639, regarded by many people as the first written constitution on this continent, setting up a definite system of government in which sovereign power was lodged with free man. They knew of the Massachusetts School Laws, 1642 and 1647—the first law dealing with education in the colonies.[20]

"More than 2400 years before the restoration of the gospel, Nephi beheld in vision the necessary prelude to that significant event: the discovery and colonization of America, the American Revolution, and the spread of the Bible" (see 1 Ne. 13:12-20, 34-37).[21] Our forefathers, the founders of this nation, openly recognized and acknowledged the hand of Providence in their writings. They laid

---

[20] Kenneth D. Wells, "Inner Man and Outer Space," Law Day, *BYU Speeches of the Year*, April 30, 1962, p. 10.

[21] Milton V. Backman Jr., "Preparing The Way: The Rise of Religious Freedom in New England," *Ensign*, Vol. 19, No. 1, January, 1989, p. 16.

a foundation for this nation that was based on limited government and a belief in God.

"From our vantage point today, we can see why it would have been difficult for a restoration to succeed until after the birth of a new nation. In addition to intolerance, the beliefs and practices of most nations were out of harmony with restoration teachings."[22]

Restoration of the Gospel

President Ezra Taft Benson explains how all this was but the essential groundwork for the next and most important event in the Lord's continuing drama for this great land:

> The establishment of this great Christian nation, with a spiritual foundation, was all in preparation for the restoration of the gospel, following the long night of apostasy. Then in 1820 the time had arrived. God the Father and his Son Jesus Christ made their glorious appearance. I give you a few words from the Prophet Joseph Smith, who was the instrument in God's hands in restoring the gospel and establishing the true Church of Christ again upon the earth. In response to humble prayer Joseph relates: "I saw a pillar of light exactly over my head, above the brightness of the sun, which descended gradually until it fell upon me.
>
> ". . . When the light rested upon me I saw two Personages, whose brightness and glory defy all description, standing above me in the air. *One of them spake unto me, calling me by name and said, pointing to the other—This is My Beloved Son. Hear Him!*" (JS–Hist. 1:16-17)
>
> To me this is the greatest event that has occurred in this world since the resurrection of the Master—*and it happened in America.*
>
> Later, other heavenly messengers came to restore the authority of the Holy Priesthood and important keys essential to the opening of the final gospel dispensation.

---

[22] *Ibid.*

The Church was organized in 1830. Immediately, in response to divine command, missionary-messengers began to carry the important message of salvation throughout the world. It is a world message intended for all of God's children. And so, once this nation was well established, then the Church was restored and from here the message of the restored gospel has gone forth. All according to divine plan.

This then becomes the Lord's *base of operations in these latter days*. And this base will not be shifted out of its place—the land of America. This nation will, in a measure at least, fulfill its mission even though it may face serious and troublesome days. The degree to which it achieves its full mission depends upon the righteousness of its people. God has, through his power, established a free people in this land as a means of helping to carry forward his purposes.

"It was his latter-day purpose to bring forth his gospel in America, not in any other place. It was in America where the Book of Mormon plates were deposited. That was no accident. It was his design. It was in this same America where they were brought to light by angelic ministry. It was [here] where he organized his modern Church, where he, himself made a modern personal appearance." (Editorial, *Church News*.) Yes, it was here under a free government and a strong nation that protection was provided for his restored Church. Now God will not permit his base of operations—America—to be destroyed. He has promised protection to this land if we will but serve the God of the land. He has also promised protection to the righteous even, if necessary, to send fire from heaven to destroy their enemies (Ether 2:12, 1 Ne. 22:17).[23]

First, let us review some of the great and glorious covenants that have been given to those who inhabit this consecrated land of promise if they will but serve the Lord.

---

[23] Ezra Taft Benson, *Conference Report*, April, 1962, p. 104 (emphasis added).

Second, we will study about those angelic visitors who restored the keys of the Dispensation of the Fullness of Times and gave other instruction to the prophet Joseph from the courts on high.

Promises to Those Who Possess This Land in Righteousness

1. It will be a land of liberty to its people.
2. They shall never be brought down into captivity (2 Ne. 1:7)
3. They shall prosper.
4. And there shall be none to molest them. (2 Ne. 1:9)
5. It is a land of promise. (1 Ne. 2:20)
6. It shall be free from all nations under heaven.
7. There shall be no enemies come into this land.
8. It shall be free from bondage. (Ether 2:12)
9. There shall be no kings upon the land. (2 Ne. 10:11)
10. I will fortify this land against all other nations (2 Ne. 10:12)
11. He that fighteth against Zion shall perish. (2 Ne. 10:13)
12. Out of Zion shall go forth the law. (Isaiah 2:3, Micah 4:1-2)

As we can clearly see, the Lord has decreed great blessings to be bestowed upon the inhabitants of this land, *but only as long as they remain righteous* and serve Him.

Personages and the Purpose of Their Appearance

The sheer number of heavenly beings who appeared to the Prophet Joseph Smith is almost beyond comprehension and thus necessitates our reviewing the nature of these visits, that we might be better able to understand the importance and magnitude of the restoration of the gospel and the attending responsibilities that were entrusted to the prophet.

1. *God the Father* opened this dispensation and introduced the Son. (JS–Hist 1:17)

2. *Jesus Christ* accepted the Kirtland Temple and directed bestowal of priesthood keys. (D&C 110:2-10)
3. *Moroni* instructed and bestowed the plates and Urim and Thummim. (JS–Hist. 1:30-49, 59)
4. *John the Baptist* conferred the Aaronic Priesthood and its keys. (D&C 13:1; HC 1:39-40)
5. *Peter, James and John* conferred the Melchizedek Priesthood and its keys. (D&C 27; HC 1:40-42)
6. *Moses* conferred the keys to gather Israel and the ten tribes. (D&C 110:11)
7. *Elias* committed the gospel of Abraham. (D&C 110:12)
8. *Elijah* conferred the sealing power. (D&C 110:13-16)
9. *Adam (Michael)* instructed Joseph. (D&C 128:21; HC 2:380; 3:388)
10. *Noah (Gabriel)* instructed Joseph. (D&C 128:21)
11. *Raphael* instructed Joseph. (D&C 128:21)
12. *Divers angels* declared their respective dispensations. (D&C 128:21)[24]
13. *Lehi* instructed Joseph. (JD 17:374)
14. *Nephi* instructed Joseph. (JD 16:266; 17:374; 21:161)
15. *Mormon* instructed Joseph. (JD 17:374)
16. *Abraham, Isaac, Jacob, Seth* and *Enoch* all communicated with Joseph but their mission is still unclear. (JD 21:94)[25]

---

[24] Bruce R. McConkie, "Divers Angels," *Ensign*, Vol. 10, No. 4, April, 1980, p. 23. Whether there may have been other angelic ministrants who restored keys and powers, we do not know. But this we do know: Every key, power, and priesthood ever held by a mortal on earth has been restored. All such came to Joseph Smith and his associates and these keys are now vested in the First Presidency and the Twelve. They lie dormant, in the sense, in all but the senior Apostle of God on earth. Since keys are the right of presidency, only one man—the President of the Church—can exercise them in their fulness at one time.

[25] See Brian L. Smith, "I Have a Question," *The Ensign*, Vol. 24, No. 10, October, 1994, p. 63. Also John Taylor, *Journal of Discourses*, April 13, 1879, Vol. 21, p. 94.

Hyrum Smith had this to say concerning his brother the prophet. *"There were prophets before, but Joseph has the spirit and power of all the prophets."*[26]

President George Q. Cannon confirmed this statement of Hyrum concerning the uniqueness of his brother, the prophet Joseph Smith:

> [Joseph] was visited constantly by angels; and the Son of God Himself condescended to come and minister unto him, the Father having also shown Himself unto him; and these various angels, the heads of dispensations, having also ministered unto him. Moroni, in the beginning, as you know, to prepare him for his mission came and ministered and talked to him from time to time, and he had vision after vision in order that his mind might be fully saturated with a knowledge of the things of God, and that he might comprehend the great and holy calling that God has bestowed upon him. *In this respect he stands unique.* There is no man in this dispensation [that] can occupy the station that he, Joseph did, God having reserved him and ordained him for that position, and bestowed upon him the necessary power.[27]

The spirit of freedom and free-market economics could only have thrived in an atmosphere such as was created here in America. The founders were "especially convinced of the need for public virtue—the willingness of each citizen to subordinate personal wants to the greater good of the community. Private and public virtue were companions. Edmund Burke wrote, 'Men are qualified for civil liberty in exact proportion to their disposition to put moral chains on their own appetites.'"[28] It has been the observance of these moral laws that has contributed to the constitutional protections enjoyed here and brought numerous blessings to this great land.

[26] Joseph Smith, *History of the Church*, Vol. 6, p. 346.

[27] George Q. Cannon, *Journal of Discourses*, October 29, 1882, Vol. 23, p. 362 (emphasis added).

[28] Lynn D. Wardle, "Seeing the Constitution as Covenant," *Ensign*, Vol. 19, No. 9, September, 1989, pp. 7-9.

There has been an explosion of religious freedom, freedom of expression, the right to assemble, the right to petition, freedom of the press, due process of law, scientific thought, inventions, technical findings, power sources such as nuclear energy, high speed transportation, communications, medical advancements, lengthening of the average life expectancy, literacy rate, and space flight.

All of this came about through the implementation of divine constitutional principles "which I [the Lord] have suffered to be established . . . according to just and holy principles . . . by the hands of wise men whom I raised up unto this very purpose." (D&C 101:77, 80)

These blessings and principles of liberty came "primarily from the swift current of freedom and prosperity which the American Founders turned loose into the spillways of human progress all over the world.

"In 200 years, the human race had made a 5,000-year leap."[29]

As we can see, major events that are crucial to the overall plans of the Lord have been reserved and foreordained to take place here, on the American continent, and there is much yet to come. It has been this chosen and consecrated land of liberty called the United States of America that the Lord has chosen to hold the banner of human liberty and religious freedom up to the entire world.

---

[29] W. Cleon Skousen, *The Five Thousand Year Leap*, pp. 1-4.

The Promised Land, an Inheritance for the House of Israel

n Deuteronomy 32 Moses tells us that Israel was in existence long before the mortal days of Abraham who was appointed to become the "father of the faithful" (D&C 138: 41) and "founder of the house of Israel" through his grandson Jacob.[1]

When the most High divided to the nations their inheritance, when he separated the sons of Adam, he set the bounds of the people according to the number of the children of Israel.

For the Lord's portion is his people; Jacob is the lot of his inheritance (Deuteronomy 32:8-9).

President Alvin R. Dyer gives the following insights into the meaning and importance of this scripture:

Members of The Church of Jesus Christ of Latter-day Saints have come to know by divine revelation in our modern time the importance of the house of Israel and its relationship to the plan of the gospel. They have come to know that the House of Israel represents the chosen of the Lord. There is a chosen people—there is a royal lineage among men here upon the earth. Many are born unto it by virtue of their premortal worthiness, and others may obtain it through adoption, by virtue of accepting the gospel here in mortality.

. . . this very important scripture teaches us that the very boundaries of every nation that has or will exist in

---

[1] Bruce R. McConkie, Compiler, *Doctrines of Salvation: Sermons and Writings of Joseph Fielding Smith*, Vol. 1, p. 184.

this world are determined as to its length of time, as to its inhabitants and that its opportunity of continuity is dependent upon the number of people who will receive the gospel, thereby establishing its boundaries by the number of children of noble lineage, either by birth or adoption, that become a part of that particular nation.

Shem, though not the eldest, was placed above Japheth and thus received the patriarchal birthright. Through the lineage of Shem has come and will continue to come the spirits of the pre-mortal estate who . . . were referred to by God as the noble and great, which is determined by fore-ordained judgment according to the eternal laws of God, of those who merit this particular earth life lineage of birth.

The genealogical record of Genesis clearly identifies Shem, the son of Noah, as the progenitor of the house of Israel or the house of God (Genesis 10:21-31), into which lineage of people are born the spirits of the pre-mortal estate who because of obedience and development in that sphere of existence merited such a mortal lineage birth.

Of this particular lineage, the Lord made a covenant with Abraham, an ethnic descendant of Shem as follows:

And in thy seed shall all the nations of the earth be blessed; because thou hast obeyed my voice. (Genesis 22:18, emphasis added)[2]

From this we can clearly see that those who are born into the lineage of Abraham, Isaac and Jacob (who was later to be called Israel), and became the progenitor of all those who were to become known as the children of Israel, were chosen to come into the world through the most distinguished lineage of any of those who were destined to come upon the earth in mortality. "Not only Israel, but all groups were thus foreknown and their total memberships designated in the pre-mortal life."[3] Israel is an eternal people that came into being before the foundations of the earth were laid; she has been in the preexistence and will

---

[2] See Alvin R. Dyer, *The Meaning of Truth*, pp. 19, 21, 37-38, 53.

[3] Bruce R. McConkie, *Mormon Doctrine*, p. 616.

continue to be here in this realm a distinct and peculiar people. The Lord said to Israel anciently: "For thou art an holy people unto the Lord thy God: the Lord thy God hath chosen thee to be a special people unto himself, above all people that are upon the face of the earth." (Deuteronomy 7:6; 14:2)

Like Shem, Ephraim was chosen by the Lord over Manasseh, who was the older, to have the birthright blessings of the first-born conferred upon him. "For the firstborn holds the right of presidency over this Priesthood, and the keys or authority of the same." (D&C 68:16-17)

Specific lands have been set aside for Israel for an inheritance in time and in eternity. (D&C 38:20) North and South America, the land of promise (1 Ne. 2:20), is the land given to the remnant of Joseph for an everlasting inheritance, the land of "everlasting hills" spoken of in the scriptures. (Genesis 49:22, 26)[4] It is from Joseph to his son Ephraim that the birthright blessings pass, and this favored status and priesthood preeminence enjoyed by Ephraim has continued to our day.

Moroni has returned to us "the keys of the record of the stick of Ephraim" (D&C 27:5) and as such he is the first to be gathered in the last days for the "richer blessings" are "upon the head of Ephraim and his fellows." (D&C 133:34) Ephraim is the tribe of service to whom the Lord is referring in the 133rd section of the Doctrine and Covenants as "my servants," and the restoration of the gospel in the Dispensation of Fulness of Times took place here in America under the direction of "Joseph Smith [who] was a pure Ephraimite."[5]

The Dispensation of the Fullness of Times

Elder David W. Patten, a member of the Quorum of the Twelve Apostles, clarified just what was to be restored in

---

[4] Erastus Snow, *Journal of Discourses*, Vol. 23, pp. 182-184. Also Orson Pratt, *Divine Authority*, No. 1 (1848), pp. 11-13.
[5] Joseph Fielding Smith, *The Way to Perfection*, p. 128.

this final great dispensation, the dispensation of the fulness of times, and thus what is meant by the term "restitution of all things" (Acts 3:20-21):

> The dispensation of the fullness of times is made up of all the dispensations that ever have been given since the world began, until this time . . . in the which all things shall be fulfilled that have been spoken of since the earth was made. . . .
>
> [Joseph Smith, the head of this dispensation] . . . must be clothed with the power of all the other dispensations, or his dispensation could not be called the dispensation of the fullness of times, for this it means, that all things shall be revealed both in heaven and on earth.[6]

Concerning the foreordained and chosen status of the Prophet Joseph Smith to usher in this final great dispensation, President Brigham Young has testified:

> It was decreed in the counsels of eternity, long before the foundations of the earth were laid, that he, Joseph Smith, should be the man, in the last dispensation of this world, to bring forth the word of God to the people, and receive the fulness of the keys and power of the Priesthood of the Son of God. The Lord had his eyes upon him, and upon his father, and upon his father's father, and upon their progenitors clear back to Abraham, and from Abraham to the flood, from the flood to Enoch, and from Enoch to Adam. He has watched that family and that blood as it has circulated from its fountain to the birth of that man. He was foreordained in eternity to preside over this last dispensation.[7]

President Heber C. Kimball testified that not only was the Prophet Joseph a literal blood descendant of Israel through Ephraim but also that Joseph "actually saw" in vision that many of the early church leaders descended

---

[6] Joseph Smith, *History of the Church*, Vol. 3, pp. 51-52.

[7] Brigham Young, *Journal of Discourses*, Vol. 7, pp. 289-290.

through a common lineage. The prophet Joseph mentioned that there were 20 or 30 other early church leaders that came down through that channel, "the aristocracy" who were also heirs of the Priesthood which came through that lineage, "all came out of one stock."[8]

Speaking to an assembly of the Saints in 1881 concerning the royal lineage of other early church leaders President Wilford Woodruff declared:

> We are called of God. We have been gathered from the distant nations, and our lives have been hid with Christ in God, but we have not known it. The Lord has been watching over us from the hour of our birth. We are of the seed of Ephraim, and of Abraham, and of Joseph, who was sold into Egypt, and these are the instruments that God has kept in the spirit world to come forth in these latter days to take hold of this kingdom and build it up.[9]

Robert L. Millet and Joseph Fielding McConkie explain how significant the blood relationship of these early leaders, through the guidance of the Lord, proved to be:

> "These declarations of relationship between the prophet's family and the Youngs and Kimballs and Richards were nothing short of prophetic," writes Archibald F. Bennett. "For in 1845 genealogical research was in its infancy, and only about thirty-six family genealogies had ever been printed in America. Heber C. Kimball had not been able to learn the names of even his grandparents, and Brigham Young knew no further than his great-grandparents. The Prophet knew back from himself five generations." (Bennett, *Saviors on Mount Zion*, p. 87.) Only recently has genealogical research been completed that verifies the claims of Joseph Smith and Brigham Young. It was long after their deaths that we learned that Joseph Smith, Oliver Cowdery, Wilford Woodruff, Parley and Orson Pratt, and Frederick G. Williams all descended from

---

[8] Heber C. Kimball, *Journal of Discourses*, Vol. 5, pp. 215-216.
[9] Wilford Woodruff, *Journal of Discourses*, Vol. 22, p. 233.

a Puritan preacher named John Lathrop. The Reverend John Lathrop had been imprisoned in England, while his wife languished at home and died. He was later allowed to bring his family to America, where he became a noted preacher. Others now established as relatives of the prophet include Heber C. Kimball, Lorenzo Snow, Willard Richards, and Franklin D. Richards. Predominant among the Prophet's forefathers were patriots, pioneers, and ministers. They ranked among the best men and women of their day. Many of his forefathers came to America seeking religious freedom; seven of them were on the Mayflower in 1620.[10]

As has been shown, the Lord has not left the great work of the restoration to chance. He has watched over and chosen the lineage of those special spirits who had proved themselves in the pre-mortal councils of heaven.

America, Chosen Location of the New Jerusalem

Preparatory to the Second Coming of the Savior, not only will America be the location of the New Jerusalem that will come down from heaven, but it also is the chosen site for The New Jerusalem or City of Zion. The City of Zion will eventually be built in Jackson County, Missouri, and a great magnificent temple of the Lord will also be constructed on this continent by a remnant of the *House of Joseph.* It shall be a land of their inheritance, and they shall build up a holy city unto the Lord (Ether 13:6-10), like unto the Jerusalem of old. This will be the capital city of the Church, the holy sanctuary. Both Enoch and Ether saw this as being built in the last days. In making this location known, the Lord said:

> Hearken, O ye elders of my Church, saith the lord your God, who have assembled yourselves together, according to my commandments, in this land, which is the land of Missouri, which is the land which I have

---

[10] Robert L. Millet & Joseph Fielding McConkie, *Our Destiny: The Call and Election of the House of Israel,* p. 54.

appointed and consecrated for the gathering of the saints. Wherefore, this is the land of promise, and the place for the city of Zion. (D&C 57:1-2)[11]

---

[11] See Bruce R. McConkie, Compiler, *Doctrines of Salvation: Sermons and Writings of Joseph Fielding Smith*, Vol. 3, pp. 66-73.

> Our nation, the United States of America, was built on the foundation of reality and spirituality. To the extent that its citizens violate God's commandments, especially His laws of morality—to that degree they weaken the country's foundation. A rejection and repudiation of God's laws could well lead our nation to its destruction just as it has to Greece and Rome. It can happen to our country unless we repent.
>
> —*Teachings of Ezra Taft Benson*, p. 571

3

The Judgments of God to Punish America

The founding of America and the restoration of the gospel were all necessary steps toward the final destiny of this great latter-day drama of the Lord.

There is a great deal of information that has been written about the future of the United States, the trials, hardships and blessings that will precede the second coming of the Savior. It appears that not only will the country be required to undergo a purification process, but the saints will as well. A cleansing must precede its ultimate glorious destiny.

Can America Escape This Destruction?

History is replete with examples of many great and powerful civilizations that have passed away because they became so immoral and degenerate that the judgments of God brought them to an end. What remains of the greatness of the Adamic-antediluvian culture, the Tower of Babel, Babylon, Nineveh, Sodom and Gomorrah, Thebes, Tyre, Carthage, Greece, Rome, the Jaredite and Nephite civilizations? All of these great empires of antiquity were renowned centers of industry, wealth, and power, and are but an example of those who have been condemned by the Lord because of their wickedness, corruption, decadence, degeneration and abominations as a nation. W. Cleon Skousen explains why an overthrow and cleansing of the godless must happen:

> When an extremely patient and long-suffering God has watched a people degrade themselves until they have

reached the point of no return, the hedonistic existence of that nation will suddenly grind to a shuddering halt through divine intervention.

No nation is immune from the administration of God's justice.

As any student of history knows, when God's judgment cleanses a nation, it often comes as an unmitigated disaster. In some cases this has been by *a surprise attack from a powerful enemy,* with burning, looting, devastation and bloodshed. At other times it has come by flood, hurricanes and earthquakes. But the most devastating of all has been by the massive affliction of an irresistible scourge of an incurable plague.

Biblical prophecy suggests that a massive, widespread affliction of consuming plagues will be the principle means by which major regions of the earth will be cleansed in the latter days [Zechariah 14:1-19; Revelation 9:20; 11:16; 15:1].

. . . History has taught us two things about great nations of the past that have been cleansed or have crumbled and disappeared into oblivion.

It appears that in each case there was a strong core of God-fearing or decent citizens—traditionally called "the remnant"—who held the shaky timbers of the collapsing nation in place much longer than the overall structure deserved. Nevertheless, the evil eventually prevailed and the inevitable collapse took place in spite of the remnant's heroic effort.

The second lesson of history tells us that when a dying political colossus collapses through a combination of war, plague, moral decay, pestilence or gigantic terrestrial disturbances, the remnant tends to survive. And even though the nation is terribly depopulated and its social structure ravaged, the loyal remnant often forms the nucleus for the new nation.

This is the prophetic destiny of the "remnant" in America.[1]

---

[1] W. Cleon Skousen, *The Majesty of God's Law,* pp. 562, 563 (emphasis added).

Alma, while prophesying to Helaman and his other sons just before he departed out of the land of Zarahemla and was taken up by the Spirit, even as Moses, made it perfectly clear that whosoever obtains this land as an inheritance must abide by His laws or be destroyed (see Alma 45:18-19).

> . . . thus saith the Lord God—Cursed shall be the land, yea, this land, unto every nation, kindred, tongue, and people, unto destruction, which do wickedly, when they are fully ripe; and as I have said so shall it be; for this is the cursing and the blessing of God upon the land, for the Lord cannot look upon sin with the least degree of allowance (Alma 45:16).

Wilford Woodruff pointed out the folly of thinking that these judgments can be avoided here in America *by anything less than the repentance of the American Nation:*

> Can the American Nation escape? The answer comes, "No." Its destruction, as well as the destruction of the world is sure; just as sure as the Lord cut off and destroyed the two great and prosperous nations that once inhabited this continent of North and South America, because of their wickedness, so will He them destroy, and sooner or later they will reap the fruits of their own wicked acts, and be numbered among the past.[2]

Our early church leaders have given us extensive written records of their discourses on these subjects as have many of our more recent church authorities. The fate, direction and ultimate destiny of this foreordained, chosen land of the Lord has always been of great interest to the members of the church. With that in mind we will start with some of the reasons that the Lord has decreed that this great land must be cleansed.

---

[2] Wilford Woodruff, *Journal of Discourses*, August 1, 1880, Vol. 21, p. 301.

Condemnation of U.S. Government

The prophet Joseph Smith explained why the condemnation of the Lord would come upon this nation if its officers did not repent:

> While discussing the petition to Congress, I prophesied, by virtue of the holy Priesthood vested in me, and in the name of the Lord Jesus Christ, that, if Congress will not hear our petition and grant us protection, they shall be broken up as a government.[3]

President Smith made a similar statement while speaking to Judge Stephen A. Douglas of the misconduct of Governor Boggs and the authorities of Missouri, who had taken part in the persecution of the Saints:

> I prophesy in the name of the Lord God of Israel, unless the United States redress the wrongs committed upon the Saints in the state of Missouri and punish the crimes committed by her officers that in a few years the government will be utterly overthrown and wasted, and there will not be so much as a potsherd left, for their wickedness in permitting the murder of men, women and children, and the wholesale plunder and extermination of thousands of her citizens to go unpunished, thereby perpetrating a foul and corroding blot upon the fair fame of this great republic, the very thought of which would have caused the high-minded and patriotic framers of the Constitution of the United States to hide their faces with shame.[4]

Speaking to the assembled Saints April 6, 1861 in the Tabernacle in Salt Lake City, President Brigham Young had this to say concerning the corruption of the government and this coming period of rioting and national disorder:

> I heard Joseph Smith say, nearly thirty years ago, "They shall have mobbing to their heart's content, if they do not redress the wrongs of the Latter-day Saints." Mobs will not

---

[3] Joseph Smith, *History of the Church*, Vol. 6, p. 116.
[4] Joseph Smith, *History of the Church*, Vol. 5, p. 394.

decrease, but will increase until the whole Government becomes a mob, and eventually it will be State against State, city against city, neighborhood against neighborhood, Methodists against Methodists, and so on.[5]

President Woodruff Sees Desolation, Disease and Strife

President Wilford Woodruff recorded in his personal journal many comments concerning the coming period of desolation, disease, internal strife and fighting of family against family. He sees much death and bloodshed that must come upon the American nation and the eventual establishment of the Kingdom of God that awaits the righteous in this generation. President Woodruff cautioned those who would later read his words to give heed concerning this future destruction and warfare that is to come upon the United States:

> I warn future historians to give credence to my history; for my testimony is true, and the truth of its record will be manifest in the world to come. All the words of the Lord will be fulfilled upon the nations, which are written in his book. The American nation will be broken in pieces like a potter's vessel, and will be cast down to hell if it does not repent—and this, because of murders, whoredoms, wickedness, and all manner of abominations, for the Lord has spoken it.[6]

The following are similar excerpts concerning this period of internal warfare that is to come upon the United States from President Woodruff's personal journal entries:

> August 7, 1847 . . . If it requires all the martyred Saints in Heaven from the righteous Able to Joseph to go forth from the temple in Heaven & pour out all the vials of the last plagues upon the United States & open the seals upon

---

[5] Brigham Young, *Journal of Discourses*, Vol. 9, p. 5.
[6] Matthias F. Cowley, *Wilford Woodruff, History of His Life and Labors*, p. 500.

them in order to avenge the blood of the Prophets & Saints which they have spilt, it will be done for that blood shall speedily be avenged. Yea very speedily.[7]

Many Great Cities to be Destroyed

July 15, 1860 . . President Young said that all that had been manifest in our day in storms, pestilence, or judgment was nothing more than a text in comparison to the sermon the Lord will preach when the Elders have finished their missions among the gentiles and are gathered with the Saints to Zion. *The Lord would open the earth & swallow up such cities as New York, Boston, Philadelphia, & other great cities of the nations and the sea would heave itself beyond its bounds and famines would spread not only over this continent and the Saints will close their eyes upon the scene and their hearts will be filled with pain.* Many remarks were made upon this subject.[8]

Breakdown of Families, Death and Disease Everywhere

December 16, 1877 . . . I went to bed at the usual hour, half past nine o'clock. I had been reading the Revelations in the French language. My mind was calm, more so than usual if that were possible. I composed myself for sleep, but could not sleep. I felt a strange stupor come over me and [I] apparently became partially unconscious. Still I was not asleep, nor awake, [but] with a strange far away dreamy feeling.

The first thing I recognized was that I was in the Tabernacle at Ogden, [Utah,] sitting on the back seat in the corner for fear they would call on me to preach,—which, after singing the second time, they did by calling me to the stand.

I arose to speak and said that I did not know that I had anything special to say except to bear my testimony of the truth of the latter-day work—when all at once it seemed as

---

[7] Susan Stoker, Editor, *Waiting For World's End: The Diaries of Wilford Woodruff*, p. 130.
[8] *Ibid.*, p. 251.

though I was lifted out of myself, and I said, "Yes, I have something to say, it is this: Some of my brethren present have been asking me what is coming to pass. . . . I will answer you right here what is coming to pass shortly.

Great Mourning Throughout the Land

I was immediately in Salt Lake City wandering about the streets in all parts of the city and on the door of every house, I found a badge of mourning, and I could not find a house but what was in mourning. I passed my own house and saw the same sign there, and asked, "is that me that is dead?" Something gave the answer, "No you'll live through it all."

It seemed strange to me that I saw no person [on] the street in my wandering about through the city. They seemed to be in their houses with their sick and dead. I saw no funeral procession, or anything of that kind, but the city looked very still and quiet as though the people were praying and had control of the disease, whatever it was.

I then looked in all directions over the territory, east, west, north and south, and I found the same mourning in every place throughout the land.

Few Men Survive the Desolation

The next I knew I was just this side of Omaha. It seemed as though I was above the earth, looking down to it as I passed along on my way east and *I saw the roads full of people, principally women, with just what they could carry in bundles on their backs traveling to the mountains on foot.* And I wondered how they could get there, with nothing but a small pack upon their backs. It was remarkable to me *that there were so few men among them.* It did not seem as though the cars were running. The rails looked rusty, and the road[s] abandoned and I have no conception [of] how I traveled myself.

As I looked down upon the people I continued eastward through Omaha and Council Bluffs, which were full of disease, and women were everywhere. The states of Missouri and Illinois were in turmoil and strife, *men killing each other, and women joining in the fight, family against family cutting each other to pieces in the most horrid manner.*

The next I saw was Washington, [D.C.], and I found the city a desolation, the White House was empty, the halls of Congress the same, *everything in ruins.* The people seemed to have fled from the city and left it to take care of itself.

I was next in the city of Baltimore, and in the square where the monument of 1812 stands in front of the St. Charles and other hotels I saw the dead piled up so high as to fill the square.

Savage, Inhuman Acts Abound

I saw mothers cut the throats of their own children for the sake of their blood, which they drank from their veins, to quench their thirst, and then lie down and die.

The waters of the Chesapeake and of the city were so stagnant and such a stench arose from them on account of the putrefaction of dead bodies that the very smell caused death and that was singular. Again I saw no men, except they were dead, lying in the streets, and very few women, and they were crazy mad, and in a dying condition. Everywhere I went I beheld the same all over the city, and it was horrible beyond description to look at.

I thought this must be the end. But no I was seemingly in Philadelphia and there everything was still. No living soul was to be seen to greet me, and it seemed as though the whole city was without an inhabitant. In Arch and Chestnut street, and in fact everywhere I went the putrefaction of the dead bodies caused such a stench that it was impossible for any creature to exist alive, nor did I see any living thing in the city.

I next found myself in Broadway New York and here it seemed the people had done their best to overcome the disease. But in wandering down Broadway, I saw the bodies of beautiful women lying stone dead, and others in a dying condition on the sidewalk. I saw men crawl out of the cellars and rob the dead bodies of the valuables they had on and before they could return to their coverts in the cellars they themselves would roll over a time or two and die in agony.

On some of the back streets *I saw mothers kill their own children and eat raw flesh*, and then in a few minutes die *themselves. Wherever I went, I saw the same scenes of horror and desolation, rapine and death*. No horses, or carriages, no buses, or streetcars, but death and destruction everywhere.

Fire, Disease and Death Engulf the Land

I then went to Grand Central Park, and looking back, I saw a fire start, and just at that moment a mighty east wind sprang up and carried the flames west over the city, and it burned until there was not a single building left standing whole; even down to the wharves. And the shipping all seemed to be burned and swallowed up in the common destruction and left nothing but a desolation where the great city was a short time before. The stench from the bodies that were burning was so great that it was carried a great distance across the Hudson River and bay, and thus spread disease and death wherever the flames penetrated.

I cannot paint in words the horrors that seemed to encompass me around. It was beyond description or thought of man to conceive.

I suppose[d] this was the end, but I was here given to understand, that the same horror was being enacted all over the country, north, south, east and west, that few were left alive. Still there were some.

Immediately after, I seemed to be standing on the west bank of the Missouri River, opposite the city of Independence, but I saw no city. *I saw the whole states of Missouri & Illinois and part of Iowa were a complete wilderness with no living human being in them.*

The Building of the New Jerusalem and Temple Begins

I then saw a short distance from the river, twelve men dressed in the robes [of] the temple, standing in a square, or nearly so. I understood it represented the twelve gates of the New Jerusalem, and they were with hands uplifted consecrating the ground and laying the cornerstones. I saw myriads of angels hovering over them and around about them and also an immense pillar of a cloud over them and I heard the singing of the most beautif[ul] music. The words [were:] *"Now is established the Kingdom of our God and His Christ and He shall reign forever and ever! And the Kingdom shall never be thrown down, for the Saints have overcome!"*

And I saw people coming from the river and different places a long way off to help build the Temple, and *it seemed that the hosts of the angels also helped to get the material to build the temple. And I saw some come who wore their Temple robes to help build the Temple and the city and all the time I saw the great pillar of cloud hovering over the place.*

Instantly I found I was in the Tabernacle at Ogden yet I could see the building going on and got quite animated in calling to the people in the tabernacle to listen to the beautiful music that the angels were making. I called to them to look at the angels as the house seemed to be full of them and they were saying the same words that I heard before: *"Now is the Kingdom of our God and His Christ established forever & ever!"*

And then a voice said "Now shall come to pass that which was spoken by Isaiah the prophet, that seven women shall take hold of one man [Isaiah 4:1]."

At this time I seemed to stagger back from the pulpit & F. D. Richards and someone else caught me and prevented me from falling when I requested Brother Richards to apologize to the audience for me because I stopped so abruptly and tell them I had not fainted but was exhausted. I rolled over in my bed and heard the city hall clock strike twelve (emphasis added).[9]

W. Cleon Skousen expresses his understanding of the above scripture in Isaiah 4:1 which states, "And in that day seven women shall take hold of one man." The reason for

---

[9] *Ibid.*, pp. 322-325.

this is explained in the previous chapter: "Thy men shall fall by the sword, and thy mighty in the war." (Isaiah 3:25) Thus we learn that this will be the necessary consequence of the great destruction and loss of life, particularly the men, that will accompany this period of time:

> At this point the vision of Isaiah is definitely pointed toward the latter days and great last cleansing of the earth prior to the Millennium. . . . Isaiah saw hosts of men hewn down and destroyed in such great numbers . . . there would be few men left. (Isaiah 3:25 commentary)

> Notice that the women in this verse consider it a "*reproach*" not to be married and have children. In periods of rebellion and unrighteousness some women want to avoid the blessings of motherhood and the joys of raising up a happy family. They say they want to be "liberated" from any such obligations. But Isaiah says that when the great wars of the latter days have destroyed millions of men, the surviving women will offer to support themselves and enter into a plurality of wives if they can have a husband and a family. Of course, the Lord forbids a plurality of wives unless it is under the patriarchal order of the Priesthood. The Lord has declared that the patriarchal order of plural marriage is specifically designed to provide superior homes for the special spirits which the Lord needs to have trained and brought up for the performance of gigantic tasks of building God's kingdom in the earth. The Lord's position is set forth by the Nephite prophet Jacob, who said: "Hearken to the word of the Lord: For there shall not any man among you have save it be one wife; and concubines he shall have none; for I, the Lord God, delight in the chastity of women. . . . If I will, saith the Lord of Hosts, raise up seed UNTO ME, I will COMMAND MY PEOPLE; otherwise they shall hearken unto these things." (Jacob 2:27-28, 30; emphasis added); [Isaiah 4:1 commentary].[10]

---

[10] W. Cleon Skousen, *Isaiah Speaks To Modern Times*, pp. 167, 170-171.

Referring to Isaiah 4:4, "When the Lord shall have washed away the filth of the daughters of Zion, and shall have purged the blood of Jerusalem from the midst thereof by the spirit of judgment, and by the spirit of burning," Dr. Skousen explains that these verses in Isaiah talk about events that will take place in both *America* and *Jerusalem:*

> Notice how Isaiah continually refers to Zion (America) and Jerusalem (the land of the Jews) together so that the reader will know that the great destruction will occur in both places. Throughout his writings he combines his observations of BOTH Zion and Jerusalem—America and Judah. In this verse he states that the daughters of Zion (*women of the Church in America, primarily*) will have been purged of their "filth," and the "spirit of judgment" and the "spirit of burning" will have purged the blood of those who have survived in Jerusalem. (Isaiah 4:4 commentary, emphasis added)[11]

It appears that during this period of time there will be a great many women of the church (*the daughters of Zion*) who will have survived during these trials and tribulations. However, since relatively few righteous men will be left alive, it may come to pass that the ordinance of patriarchal plural marriage may be re-instituted under the consent and direction of the Almighty. Because there may be so many more righteous women than men, this may be the only way that they will be able to belong to a righteous family organization. It is quite possible that plural marriage, established by the Lord through His priesthood, may become a necessity of life.

It Will Be Family Against Family

The Prophet Joseph Smith tells us of the terrible destruction of life and property that will result from the mobbings of those who have lost the spirit of the Lord and have

---

[11] *Ibid.,* p. 173.

been overtaken by the spirit and rage of the devil during this period of time:

> I saw men hunting the lives of their own sons, and brother murdering brother, women killing their own daughters, and daughters seeking the lives of their mothers. I saw armies arrayed against armies. I saw blood, desolation, fires. The Son of man has said that the mother shall be against the daughters, and the daughter against the mother. These things are at our doors. They will follow the Saints of God from city to city. Satan will rage, and the spirit of the devil is now enraged. I know not how soon these things will take place; but with a view of them, shall I cry peace? No; I will lift up my voice and testify of them. How long you will have good crops, and the famine be kept off, I do not know; when the fig tree leaves, know then that the summer is nigh at hand.[12]

But in this context, it is good to remember the observation of the prophet Nephi: "Wherefore, the righteous need not fear" (1 Nephi 22:17).

---

[12] Joseph Fielding Smith, Compiler, *Teachings of the Prophet Joseph Smith*, p. 161.

And it shall come to pass in the last days that the mountain of the Lord's house shall be established in the top of the mountains, and shall be exalted above the hills; and all nations shall flow unto it.

—Isaiah 2:2

The Rocky Mountains: A Place of Refuge for the Saints

President Brigham Young also described how the Lord had prepared a special place, a refuge, a place of peace and safety for His righteous Saints. There they would be hid up and protected from the coming storms of violence, disorder and destruction that are destined to descend upon this nation because of its iniquity and refusal to repent:

> It [these mountains] *has been designed for many generations to hide up the Saints in the last days until the indignation of the Almighty be over. . . . We are blessed in these mountains. Here is the place in which the Lord designed to hide his people.*[1]

Heber C. Kimball also agreed that these mountains were "foreordained to be the gathering place of the Saints, where the Lord would hide up his people until his indignation should pass over the nations of the earth."[2]

Will the Elders of Israel Save the Constitution from Destruction?

In the June, 1976 issue of the *Ensign*, D. Michael Stewart of the Brigham Young University Department of History gave the following explanation of just what we do know

---

[1] Brigham Young, *Journal of Discourses*, April 6, 1861, Vol. 9, pp. 2-3 (emphasis added).
[2] Heber C. Kimball, *Journal of Discourses*, April 14, 1861, Vol. 9, p. 52.

concerning the Prophet Joseph Smith's purported statement that the *Constitution would hang by a thread and
that the elders would save it:*

> The first known record of the prophecy dates to July 19,
> 1840, in Nauvoo, when the prophet spoke about the
> redemption of Zion. Using Doctrine & Covenants 101 as a
> text, he said, "Even this nation will be on the verge of
> crumbling to pieces and tumbling to the ground and when
> the Constitution is on the brink of ruin this people will be
> the staff upon which the nation shall lean and they shall
> bear the Constitution away from the very verge of destruc-
> tion." (Joseph Smith Papers, LDS Church Historical
> Archives, Box 1, March 10, 1844.)

> There are also other documents in Church History files
> that show that five different early Saints recorded some
> remarks by the Prophet Joseph Smith on the same
> prophecy, perhaps voiced by the Prophet a number of
> times in a number of ways after 1840. Parley P. Pratt wrote
> in 1841 that the prophet said, "The government is fallen
> and needs redeeming. It is guilty of *Blood* and cannot
> stand as it now is but will come so near desolation as to
> hang as it were by a single hair! Then the servants goes
> [sic] to the nations of the earth, and gathers the strength
> of the Lord's house! A mighty army! *And this is the redemp-
> tion of Zion when the saints shall have redeemed that gov-
> ernment and reinstated it in all its purity and glory!* (George
> A. Smith Papers, Church Archives, Box 7, Folder 5, Janu-
> ary 21, 1841.)

> James Burgess related that the Prophet, while
> addressing the Nauvoo Legion several miles east of Nau-
> voo in May 1843, said that "the time would come when
> the constitution and government would hang by a brittle
> thread and would be ready to fall into other hands but
> this people the latter-day saints will step forth and save
> it." (James Burgess Journal, 1818-1904, Church
> Archives, Vol. 1—found among loose sermons.)

> . . . On various occasions, Joseph Smith referred to the
> Constitution, the country, and destiny of the nation; and

there is clear evidence that he anticipated future peril. Furthermore, he pronounced the prophecy at various times and places. Perhaps he himself interchanged the simile "on the brink of ruin," "hang by a thread," "hang by a single hair," etc., to describe the anticipated crisis. *It is also clear that the redeemers or rescuers of the Constitution were to be either the Saints generally or priesthood officers specifically.*

. . . The prophecy clearly indicates a *single, identifiable episode yet to come.*[3]

Orson Hyde gave this clarification of some of the statements attributed to the Prophet Joseph Smith concerning the role that the Elders of Israel would play in stepping forward and rescuing the constitution from threatened destruction:

It is said that brother Joseph in his lifetime declared that the Elders of this Church should step forth at a particular time when the Constitution should be in danger, and rescue it, and save it. This may be so; but I do not recollect that he said exactly so. I believe he said something like this—that the time would come when the Constitution and the country would be in danger of an overthrow; and said he, if the Constitution be saved at all, it will be by the Elders of this Church. I believe this is about the language, as nearly as I can recollect it.[4]

Heber C. Kimball was another who felt that the members of the church would play an important role in the perpetuation of our constitutional form of government:

We will yet save the Constitution of the United States. We will do it, as the Lord liveth, and we will save this nation, every one of them that will be saved. Brother

---

[3] D. Michael Stewart, "I Have a Question: What do we know about the purported statement of Joseph Smith that the Constitution would hang by a thread and that the Elders would save it?" *Ensign*, Vol. 6, No. 6, June, 1976, pp. 64-65 (emphasis added).

[4] Orson Hyde, *Journal of Discourses*, Vol. 6, January 3, 1858, p. 152.

Brigham Young and Brother Joseph Smith stand at our head, and will do that thing, as the Lord liveth. Yes, we, as their children, with our children to assist us, will do it. We have got that power, and so have they, and will bear the kingdom off victoriously to every nation that is upon God's footstool; and I know it.[5]

President Ezra Taft Benson also held a firm conviction that the Elders of the church, the priesthood, would at some point respond unitedly and rally the country behind the principles of constitutional government.

> I have faith that the Constitution will be saved, as prophesied by Joseph Smith. It will be saved by the right-eous citizens of this nation who love and cherish freedom. *It will be saved by the enlightened members of this Church—among others—men and women who understand and abide the principles of the Constitution.*
>
> The Lord told the Prophet Joseph Smith there would be an attempt to overthrow the country by destroying the Constitution. Joseph Smith predicted that the time would come when the Constitution would hang, as it were, by a thread, and at that time "this people will step forth and save it from the threatened destruction" (*Journal of Discourses* 7:15). It is my conviction that the elders of Israel, widely spread over the nation, will at that crucial time successfully rally the righteous of our country and provide the necessary balance of strength to save the institutions of constitutional government.[6]

President Ezra Taft Benson also warned of the danger of the priesthood not taking their responsibilities seriously and being lulled to sleep by the deceptions of Satan:

> The devil knows that if the elders of Israel should ever wake up, they could step forth and help preserve freedom

---

[5] Heber C. Kimball, *Journal of Discourses*, Vol. 5, September 6, 1856, p. 216.

[6] Ezra Taft Benson, *Teachings of Ezra Taft Benson*, pp. 622, 618-619 (emphasis added).

and extend the gospel. Therefore the devil has concentrated, and to a large extent successfully, on neutralizing much of the priesthood. He has reduced them to sleeping giants.[7]

President John Taylor, while speaking of this, explains:

The Elders of Israel will step forth *to save the constitutional principles set forth in the constitution rather than the actual government itself.*

When the people have torn to shreds the Constitution of the United States the Elders of Israel will be found holding it up to the nations of the earth and proclaiming liberty and equal rights to all men, and extending the hand of fellowship to the oppressed of all nations.[8]

In his personal journal Mosiah Hancock listed many things that he attributed to the Prophet Joseph Smith when he was visiting him in his home. Among them were these statements concerning the future destiny and tribulation period that is to come upon the United States:

The United States will spend her strength and means warring in foreign lands until other nations will say, "Let's divide up the lands of the United States," then the people of the U.S. will unite and swear by the blood of their forefathers, that the land shall not be divided. Then the country will go to war, *and they will fight until one half of the U.S. army will give up,* and the rest will continue to struggle. They will keep on until they are very ragged and discouraged, and almost ready to give up—*when the boys from the mountains will rush forth in time to save the American army from defeat and ruin.* And they will say, 'Brethren, we are glad you have come; give us men, henceforth, who can talk with God.' Then you will have friends,

---

[7] *Ibid.*, p. 659.
[8] John Taylor, *Journal of Discourses*, Vol. 21, August 31, 1879, p. 8 (emphasis added).

but you will save the country when its liberty hangs by a hair, as it were.[9]

Orson Pratt also felt that the United States would become incapable of governing in the chaos that will beset this nation. He believed that it would be at this time when the members of the church would step forward and fulfill their foreordained mission to preserve the spirit of the Constitution. Speaking of the Lord he said that:

> He will speedily fulfill the prophecy in relation to the overthrow of this nation, and their destruction. We shall be obliged to have a government to preserve ourselves in unity and peace; for they, through being wasted away, will not have power to govern; for state will be divided against state, city against city, town against town, and the whole country will be in terror and confusion; mobocracy will prevail and there will be no security, through this great Republic, for the lives or property of the people.
>
> *When that time shall arrive, we shall necessarily want to carry out the principles of our great constitution and, as the people of God, we shall want to see those principles magnified, according to the order of union and oneness which prevails among the people of God.*[10]

In 1855 President Brigham Young, speaking to the Saints concerning the destiny of this great nation in the Tabernacle in Salt Lake City, had this to say:

> When the day comes in which the Kingdom of God will bear rule, the flag of the United States will proudly flutter unsullied on the flag staff of liberty and equal rights, without a spot to sully its fair surface; the glorious flag our fathers have bequeathed to us will then be unfurled to the

---

[9] Mosiah Lyman Hancock, *The Journal of Mosiah Hancock*, p. 19-20. Also Amy E. Baird, Victory H. Jackson, and Laura L. Wassell, Compilers, *Mosiah Lyman Hancock (1834-1907) Autobiography (1834-1865)*, p. 29 (emphasis added).

[10] Orson Pratt, *Deseret Evening News*, Vol. 8, No. 265, October 2, 1875 (emphasis added).

breeze by those who have power to hoist it aloft and defend its sanctity.[11]

Christ's government will be a theocracy, which means literally "God rule." In 1859, from the same pulpit in the Tabernacle, President Young clarified what he meant when using the terms "theocratic government" or "the kingdom of God:"

> When the kingdom of God is established upon the earth, people will find it to be very different from what they now imagine. Will it be in the least degree tyrannical and oppressive towards any human being? No, it will not; for such is not the kingdom of God.
>
> . . . What do I understand by a theocratic government? One in which all laws are enacted and executed in right-eousness, and whose officers possess that power which proceedeth from the Almighty. That is the kind of government I allude to when I speak of a theocratic government, or the kingdom of God upon the earth. It is, in short, the eternal powers of the Gods.
>
> . . . *Few if any, understand what a theocratic government is. In every sense of the word, it is a republican government*, and differs but little in form from our National, State, and Territorial Governments; but its subjects will recognize the will and dictation of the Almighty!
>
> . . . *The constitution and laws of the United States resemble a theocracy more closely than any government now on the earth* . . .[12]

Supporting this definition of the kingdom of God, President Joseph F. Smith had this to say: "What I mean by the kingdom of God is the organization of the Church of Jesus Christ of Latter-day Saints, over which the Son of God presides, and not man."[13]

---

[11] Brigham Young, *Journal of Discourses*, Vol. 2, July 8, 1855, p. 317.

[12] Brigham Young, *Journal of Discourses*, Vol. 6, July 31, 1859, pp. 342-349 (emphasis added).

[13] Joseph F. Smith, *Gospel Doctrine*, p. 72.

From the foregoing quotations it sounds like the current government of the United States, as it is now constituted, will be brought down to its knees by the judgments of God, just as the once-great Jaredite and Nephite nations were destroyed or very nearly so. However, as the Prophet Joseph stated, the elders of Israel will at some point step forward under divine guidance to provide the leadership necessary to rescue, redeem and reinstate it "in all its purity and glory."[14] The Saints will step forward at this crucial juncture to uphold and maintain these heavenly inspired principles of our country as they were originally set forth by the Lord. We will take these honored principles of inspired government with us when we go back to Jackson County, Missouri to build the temple. We will revere and hold up these principles to all other nations as a standard of freedom that has come forth from the Lord. "The Kingdom of God" will "bear rule" and flow from the New Jerusalem under a constitutional republican form of government until the Lord comes and replaces it with a theocracy under His personal direction and reign. The flag of the United States will "be unfurled" and fly again as the symbol of freedom, liberty and equal rights from the New Jerusalem, as this is where the Kingdom of God will have its headquarters and send out the law to the world.

Jackson County and the New Jerusalem

In a sermon delivered in the 16th Ward Assembly Rooms in Salt Lake City, Elder Orson Pratt had this to say about Jackson County and the glory of the City of Zion or New Jerusalem which is to built there:

> We shall erect in that county a beautiful city after the order and pattern that the Lord shall reveal, part of which has already been revealed. God intends to have a city built up that will never be destroyed nor overcome, but that will

---

[14] D. Michael Stewart, "I Have a Question: What do we know about the purported statement of Joseph Smith that~the Constitution would hang by a thread and that the Elders would save it?" *Ensign*, Vol. 6, No. 6, pp. 64-65.

exist while eternity shall endure; and he will point out the pattern and show the order of architecture; he will show unto his servants the nature of the streets and the pavement thereof, the kind of precious stones that shall enter into the buildings, the nature of the rock and precious stones that will adorn the gates and the walls of that city; for the gates will be open continually says the Prophet Isaiah, that men may bring in the force of the Gentiles.[15]

The New Jerusalem to Be a Place of Safety

Do we know what kind of a place this great city will be, and who will be allowed to come there? Will the righteous look upon it any differently than the wicked of the world? In answering these questions Hugh Nibley points out that:

> In the first place, we are told, it will be a place of refuge in a doomed world, "and it shall be called the New Jerusalem, a land of peace, a city of refuge, a place of safety for the saints of the Most High God; . . . and the terror of the Lord also shall be there . . . and it shall be called Zion" (D & C 45:66-67). At that time, "every man that will not take his sword against his neighbor must needs flee unto Zion for safety. . . . And it shall be said among the wicked . . . the inhabitants of Zion are terrible" (D&C 45:68, 70). Terrible because it is indestructible. Her invulnerability makes her an object of awe and terror.
>
> . . . "The gathering together upon the land of Zion, and upon her stakes, may be for a defense, and for a refuge from the storm, and from wrath when it shall be poured out without mixture upon the whole earth" (D&C 115:6). It would seem that Zion enjoys the complete security of the celestial world, and nothing can touch it as long as it retains that character. But celestial it must be. We have seen that "Zion cannot be built up unless it is by the principles of the law of the celestial kingdom; otherwise I cannot receive her unto myself" (D&C 105:5). It must at all times be holy enough to receive the Lord himself, "for the Lord hath chosen Zion; he hath desired it for his

---

[15] Orson Pratt, *Journal of Discourses*, Vol. 15, March 9, 1873, p. 365.

habitation" (Psalms 132:13). There is no place for those who promote themselves "to honor and glory by deceitful practices, who misapply and misinterpret straightforward statements, who have given a new twist to the everlasting covenant and then produce arguments to prove that you are without guilt." That is from the very valuable Greek Enoch, discovered in 1930. Enoch explains that all this self-deception is really quite stupid; it leads to self-destruction (D&C 99:5).[16]

From revelation given to Joseph Smith the Prophet, we find that the city of Zion and the New Jerusalem are one and the same. There are a number of revelations where the Lord speaks of the New Jerusalem which is to be built in the latter-days (see D&C 45:66-67).

So, as we can see, the wicked and evil of the world will want nothing to do with the city Zion in these days. Because of its glory, grandeur, beauty, magnificence, power and the speed with which this great city will be built, they will recognize that it is the power and strength of the Lord that protects and defends it. They will be perfectly aware that it is His glory that visibly radiates from it. Because of the strength, power and authority that emanate from this great city, the wicked and corrupt will be perfectly satisfied to observe its beauty and glory from afar. No doubt the rapid growth of the city and enormous concentration of the virtuous and righteous saints in this one place will create an uneasiness in the wicked that will be very unsettling, aggravating, and disturbing to the point that it will indeed strike them with terror.

It becomes very apparent that the building of the city of Zion will be the key to the preservation and protection of the saints in the last days. It will be the only place on earth that the Saints will be shielded from the calamities that "shall be poured out without mixture upon the whole earth" (D&C 115:6).

---

[16] Hugh Nibley, *Collected Works of Hugh Nibley: Approaching Zion*, Vol. 9, pp. 319-321.

Various Dreams and Visions
Concerning This
Latter-day Period of Strife

There are a number of comparable dreams and visions that have been reported by various non-Mormons, as well as members of the Church, that are not from our church leadership, concerning this latter-day period of time and the American Nation. They come from the general membership of the Church as well as those from other religious and social backgrounds, from across this country and others.

However, they are very interesting because of their similarities. They are not to be considered infallible, and are to be looked upon only as interesting reading that correlates quite well with many of the statements our church leaders have made and how the spirit of the Lord descends on many of his children. Taken together they show future events ranging from the beginning trials of this nation to its fall, and the eventual rise of the New Jerusalem. The author felt it would be of interest to compile some of the similar dreams and statements made by those both in and out of the Church so that they could be easily compared. They are for you to read and discern their value by the power and inspiration of the Holy Ghost. This author has corrected minor spelling errors, emphasized certain verses in the text and added sub-headings. Some of them will be in their entirety, while others will only quote that part which is pertinent to our discussion and review of this future period of time.

Vision of General George Washington

General George Washington had this vision during the Revolutionary War, in 1777, at Valley Forge. Washington told a young soldier by the name of Anthony Sherman of his vision. The dream, as related by Sherman, was published by Wesley Bradshaw about 1859 and later reprinted in *The National Tribune*, Vol. 4, No. 12, December, 1880:

> The last time I ever saw Anthony Sherman was on the fourth of July, 1859, in Independence Square. He was then 99 years old, and becoming very feeble; but though so old, his dimming eyes rekindled as he gazed upon Independence Hall, which he had come to gaze upon once more before he was gathered home.

> "Let us go into the hall," he said, "I want to tell you an incident of Washington's life—one which no one alive knows of except myself, and if you live, you will before long see it verified. Mark the prediction, you will see it verified.

General Washington Kneels in Prayer

> "From the opening of the Revolution we experienced all phases of fortune—now good and now ill, one time victorious and another conquered. The darkest period we had, I think, was when Washington, after several reverses, retreated to Valley Forge, where he resolved to pass the winter of 1777. Ah! I have often seen the tears coursing down our dear old commander's careworn cheeks as he would be conversing with a confidential officer about the condition of his poor soldiers. You have doubtless heard the story of Washington going to the thicket to pray. Well, it was not only true, but he used often to pray in secret for aid and comfort from God, the interposition of whose Divine Providence brought us safely through those dark days of tribulation.

> "One day, I remember it well, the chilly winds whistled through the leafless trees, though the sky was cloudless and the sun shone brightly; he remained in his quarters nearly all the afternoon alone. When he came out I noticed his face was a shade paler than usual and there seemed

to be something on his mind of more than ordinary importance. Returning just after dusk, he dispatched an orderly to the quarters of the officer I mentioned, who was presently in attendance. After a preliminary conversation, which lasted about half an hour, Washington, gazing upon his companion with that strange look of dignity which he alone could command, said to the latter:

A Vision of America's Future

"I do not know whether it is owing to the anxiety of my mind, or what, but this afternoon as I was sitting at this very table engaged in preparing a dispatch, something in the apartment seemed to disturb me. Looking up, I beheld standing opposite to me a singularly beautiful female. So astonished was I, for I had given strict orders not to be disturbed, that it was some moments before I found language to inquire the cause of her presence. A second, a third, and even a fourth time did I repeat my question, but received no answer from my mysterious visitor except a slight raising of the eyes. By this time I felt strange sensations spreading through me. I would have risen, but the riveted gaze of the being before me rendered volition impossible. I assayed once more to address her, but my tongue had become powerless. Even thought itself suddenly became paralyzed. A new influence, mysterious, potent, irresistible, took possession of me. All I could do was to gaze steadily, vacantly, at my unknown visitant. Gradually the surrounding atmosphere seemed as though becoming filled with sensations and grew luminous. Everything about me seemed to rarify, the mysterious visitor herself becoming more airy, and yet more distinct to my sight than before. I now began to feel as one dying—or rather to experience the sensations which I have sometimes imagined accompany dissolution. I did not think, I did not reason, I did not move; all were alike impossible. I was only conscious of gazing fixedly, vacantly at my companion.

"Presently I heard a voice saying, 'Son of the republic, look and learn,' while at the same time my visitor extended her arm eastwardly. I now beheld a heavy white vapor at some distance rising fold upon fold. This gradually dissipated, and I looked upon a strange scene. Before me lay spread out in one vast plain all the countries of the world—Europe, Asia, Africa, and America. I saw rolling and tossing between Europe and America the billows of the Atlantic, and between Asia and America lay the Pacific. 'Son of the Republic,' said the same mysterious voice as before, 'look and learn.' At that moment I beheld a dark, shadowy being, like an angel standing, or, rather, floating, in mid-air, between Europe and America. Dipping water out of the ocean in the hollow of each hand, he sprinkled some upon America with his right hand, while with his left hand he cast some upon Europe. Immediately a dark cloud raised from each of these countries and joined in mid ocean. For a while it remained stationary, and then moved slowly westward, until it enveloped America in its murky folds. Sharp flashes of lighting gleamed through it at intervals, and I heard the smothered groans and cries of the American people. A second time the angel dipped water from the ocean and sprinkled it out as before. The dark cloud was then drawn back to the ocean, in whose heaving waves it sank from view. A third, I heard the mysterious voice saying: 'Son of the Republic, look and learn.' I cast my eyes upon America and beheld villages and towns and cities springing up one after another, until the whole land from the Atlantic to the Pacific was dotted with them. Again, I heard the mysterious voice say 'Son of the Republic, the end of the Century cometh; look and learn.'

The U.S. Civil War Foreseen

"At this the dark shadowy angel turned his face southward, and from Africa I saw an ill-omened specter approach our land. It flitted slowly and heavily over town and city of the latter; the inhabitants presently set themselves in battle array against each other. As I continued looking I saw a bright angel, on whose brow rested a crown of light, on which was traced 'Union,' bearing the American flag, which was placed between the divided nation, and said: 'Remember, ye are brethren.' Instantly the inhabitants, casting from them their weapons, became friends once more and united around the National Standard.

America to Be Invaded by Foreign Powers

"And again I heard the mysterious voice saying: 'Son of the Republic, the end of the century cometh; look and learn.' At this the dark shadowy angel placed a trumpet to his mouth and blew three distinct blasts, and taking water from the ocean, he sprinkled it upon Europe, Asia, and Africa. Then my eyes beheld a fearful scene. From each of these countries arose thick black clouds that were soon joined into one. And throughout this mass there gleamed a dark red light, by which I saw hordes of armed men, who, moving with the cloud, marched by land and sailed by sea to America, which country was enveloped in the volume of the cloud. And I dimly saw these vast armies devastate the whole country and burn the villages, towns and cities that I beheld springing up. As my ears listened to the thundering of the cannon, clashing of swords, and the shouts and cries of millions in mortal combat, I again heard the mysterious voice saying,: 'Son of the Republic, look and learn.'

"When the voice had ceased the dark shadowy angel placed his trumpet once more to his mouth, and blew a long, powerful blast.

With Divine Intervention America Is Victorious

"Instantly a light, as if of a thousand suns, shone down from above me, and pierced and broke into fragments the dark cloud which enveloped America. At the same moment the angel upon whose head still shone the word 'Union,' and who bore our national flag in one hand and a sword in the other, descended from heaven attended by legions of bright spirits.

"These immediately joined the inhabitants of America, who, I perceived, were well nigh overcome, but who, immediately taking courage again, closed up their broken ranks and renewed the battle. Again, amid the fearful noise of the conflict, I heard the mysterious voice saying: 'Son of the Republic, look and learn.'

"As the voice ceased, the shadowy angel for the last time dipped water from the ocean and sprinkled it upon America. Instantly the dark cloud rolled back, together with the armies it had brought, leaving the inhabitants of the land victorious.

"Then, once more, I beheld villages, towns, and cities springing up where they had been before, while the bright angel, planting the azure standard he had brought in the midst of them, cried with a loud voice: 'While the stars remain and the heavens send down dew upon the earth, so long shall the Republic last.' And taking from his brow the crown, on which blazoned the word 'Union' he placed it upon the standard, while the people, kneeling down, said 'Amen.'

"The scene instantly began to fade and dissolve, and I at last saw nothing but the rising, curling vapor I had at first beheld. This also disappearing, I found myself once more gazing on my mysterious visitor, who, in the same voice I heard before, said: '*Son of the Republic, what ye have seen is thus interpreted: Three great perils will come upon the Republic. The most fearful is second, passing which the whole world united shall never be able to prevail against her. Let every child of the Republic learn to live for his God, his land, and Union.*'

"With these words the vision vanished, and I started from my seat and felt that I had seen a vision wherein had been shown me the birth, progress, and destiny of the United States. *In union she will have her strength, in disunion her destruction.*

"Such, my friends," concluded the venerable narrator, "were the words I heard from Washington's own lips, and America will do well to profit by them."

—Wesley Bradshaw[1]

It has been reported that Washington's vision was first published in 1859, however, the author has not been able to find a copy of the original from that year. The above copy of General George Washington's Dream was taken directly from a microfilm copy of the original December, 1880 edition of *The National Tribune*. The dream was reprinted from a copy of the original which was furnished by someone referred to only as J.W.H. He obtained the copy from his neighbor in response to a request from a reader.

There appear to be a number of variations of this dream in circulation. Most copies mention a "singularly beautiful being" in reference to the heavenly personage that appeared to Washington rather than a "singularly beautiful female" that he beheld standing opposite him. Most copies state that the most fearful peril was the third, however, the 1880 edition of the dream clearly spells out "the most fearful is [the] second." Most copies also exclude the last sentence of the next to the last paragraph in the vision; "In union she will have her strength, in disunion her destruction." This significant statement would lend strength to the second peril being the most dangerous one: civil war among the inhabitants of this nation or "disunion." It is very apparent that the unity of the nation and people are a very important part of the message that was conveyed to Washington from the angel. Remember, Washington stated that he saw "a bright angel, on whose brow rested *a crown of light, on which was traced "Union."* The angel then cautions the fighting inhabitants of a divided nation, "*Remember, ye are brethren.*" Later in the vision Washington describes "*the angel upon whose head still*

---

[1] Wesley Bradshaw, as told by Anthony Sherman and published in *The National Tribune*, Vol. 4, No. 12, December 1880, p. 1 (emphasis added).

shone the word "Union" to be carrying our *national flag* and leading "legions of bright spirits" in defense of America's inhabitants. This heavenly being then declares *"While the stars remain and the heavens send down dew upon the earth, so long shall the Republic last. And taking from his brow the crown, on which blazoned the word 'Union' he placed it upon the standard [the flag] while the people, kneeling down, said 'Amen.'"* After warning Washington of the three perils that would beset this nation the "mysterious visitor" then gave this admonition "Let every child of the Republic learn to live for his God, his land, and Union."

When the angel had finished the narrative, Washington's impression was that he had been shown the birth, progress and destiny of the United States. He then gave this synopsis of what he had seen with this final warning to the nation. *"In union she will have her strength, in disunion her destruction."* This also appears to be a very key phrase if we expect to clearly understand the prophesies of Joseph Smith in which he describes a future period of national discord, disunion and destabilization among the communities and inhabitants of this land. This threat to the very existence of our country will finally be overcome, but only when the divine intervention of heaven comes to the aid of the inhabitants of this nation.

There are also a number of other smaller differences that this author has found in later copies, but the 1880 edition appears to be one of the oldest and therefore must be considered to be more accurate than many of the later versions.

Another Civil War Predicted

The Lord has used civil war to cleanse this nation of two great civilizations. The Jaredites and Nephites were utterly destroyed as nations and swept off the face of the land because of their iniquities.

Although America was divided during the Civil War, it was *reunited* when the northern states (*the Union forces*) won the conflict. The country subsequently went on to become the greatest nation and ensign for liberty the world has ever seen. It has been this unparalleled union of diversity, people, cultures, and states that has indeed given America much of "her strength." However, it appears that an invading foreign power coupled with the internal chaos and strife that will afflict the inhabitants of the United States in the future will destabilize the union and oneness of the country and thus may also fulfill Washington's words of warning, "*in disunion her destruction.*"

The breakdown of the federal government will cause internal strife that will devastate this country. There will be mobocracy and bloodshed such as has never been seen before. The result of such mobocracy and bloodshed will be "a war of neighborhood against neighborhood, *city against city, town against town, county against county, state against state, and they will go forth destroying and being destroyed.*"[2]

There is an increasing number of analysts and military theorists who have independently developed similar lines of thought concerning a coming disintegration and decentralization of American society. One of these, Thomas Chittum, foresees just such a breakdown of the American Union in his book *Civil War Two: The Coming Breakup of America.* Chittum served a number of years in the Army in Vietnam and currently writes a weekly column that examines current events from the perspective of another possible civil war. Chittum says that current economic, social and political forces are tearing America apart and propelling her toward a bloody war that may divide the country into several different warring factions. These factions will be created along ethnic lines. Falling wages, rising unemployment, riots, gangs and militias are all circumstances that will add fuel to this expanding movement:

> America was born in blood. America suckled on blood. America gorged on blood and grew into a giant, and America will drown in blood. This is the spectre that

---

[2] Orson Pratt, *Journal of Discourses*, Vol. 20, p. 151 (emphasis added).

is haunting America, the spectre of Civil War II, a second civil war that will shatter America into several new
ethnically-based nations . . . Simply and directly put,
America will explode in tribal warfare in our lifetime. . . .
Bands of guerrillas will stalk about the countryside—
raping, looting, murdering, clashing with each other.

. . . Civil War II in America will set off a super depression that will plunge the entire globe into economic chaos,
which will further deepen the economic collapse here in
America.

Food production will all but cease. The hungry will fight
to the death over scraps of garbage. Millions will starve,
and millions more will die from infectious diseases. Behold
the vision of Civil War II.

. . . Depending on the scope and duration of Civil War
II, tens of millions could perish in a mass starvation
unprecedented since the beginning of time. Millions more
will die of disease due to immune systems weakened by
lack of food. The very old and children will die off first. Soldiers, the most valuable and most heavily-armed portion
of the population, will suffer the least.

. . . Western Civilization will be transformed; tribalism
will blossom into its ultimate expression. . . . And what
excuse will we Americans have? . . . *that no one cautioned
us that a house divided against itself cannot stand*?[3]

This destabilization of the American union will reach all
the way down to the disintegration of its most common
denominator of stability, the family. It will be a time when
men will seek the lives of their own sons, and brother will
be against brother. There will be "women killing their own
daughters and daughters seeking the lives of their mothers."[4] The fighting between the various factions will mirror
the horrors of the Civil War of 1860-1865 when family
fought against family. Only this time it will be much more
destructive and inhuman as the spirit of the Lord will have

[3] Thomas W. Chittum, *Civil War Two: The Coming Breakup of America*, pp. 1, 83, 84, 196, 197 (emphasis added).
[4] Joseph Fielding Smith, *Teachings of the Prophet Joseph Smith*,
p. 161.

been totally withdrawn and there will be no quarter given to even the women, the children, or the disabled and aged as there was in the earlier conflict. Death, desolation and destruction will reign supreme and the blood and unentombed bodies of the dead will cover this land again unless the people of this nation repent.[5]

Vision of Mrs. Sols Guardisto

While not a member of the LDS Church, Mrs. Sols Guardisto, a Quaker and magazine writer, was given a similar vision of the latter-day, pre-millennium period of great destruction spoken of by various of our church leaders. She was visiting in Cardston, Alberta, Canada while the Cardston temple was under construction, and received these promptings while being escorted on two tours of the site in progress. She describes visions of world-wide devastation and the death of people on a massive scale. Mrs. Guardisto describes a war that began upon the Pacific Ocean and was divided by the forces of *Christianity* on one side and the followers of *Mohammed* and *Buddha* on the other, in which chaos, hunger and rioting followed. She was made aware of the Church being led spiritually, by former leaders, in the creation of a great place of refuge from the coming storm. They were preparing the area, stockpiling necessities and organizing the Saints to make the necessary preparations to survive a coming time of destruction. While this vision or dream is not to be looked upon as doctrine in any way, the similarities to our own beliefs are very striking, and interesting comparisons can be made by the reader:

Mrs. Guardisto Prompted to Record Her Vision

We have been in the temple erected by your church, wherein the sacred rites are to be performed in accordance with your faith. *The first time I was strongly impelled to describe to you my impressions.*

---

[5] See Joseph Fielding Smith, *The Signs of the Times*, p. 131. Also Jerrell L. Newquist, *Gospel Truth: Discourses and Writings of President George Q. Cannon*, Vol. 2, pp. 343-351.

. . . For never before in my life have such powerful impressions been impinged upon my inner consciousness as during my visits through the temple, especially was this so at our second visit: the impressions of our first visit were repeated with such overwhelming intensity and variety of detail *that I must positively inform you of my experiences.*

It seems to me it were a sacred duty upon my part to do so.

. . . Every now and again I would seem to receive a command, "*observe, remember and record,*" and vivid as all of it was, these incidents herein related *are the ones upon which I received the instructions.*

. . . It seemed as though the temple was filled with the actual spiritual bodies of these previous leaders of your church, each seeming to have a definite work to do, automatically taking up in the spirit world the work that person was engaged in whilst in the flesh. In that temple I saw persons who were leaders of your church, during its march across the American desert, now engaged in helping these higher patriarchs under whose orders they seemed to be working. *It was these latter spiritual leaders, if I may use that term, who seemed to be instructed to show me the scenes here recorded.*

I can give no time as to the happenings, except that the impressions I received were of actual present or immediate future.

I saw first a brief but comprehensive sketch of the present state of the world, or as you would term it, the Gentile Kingdoms. Each country in turn was shown, its anarchy, hunger, ambitions, distrusts and warlike activities, etc., and in my mind was formed from some source the words, "As it is today with the Gentiles."

A World-Wide War Begins

I saw next, international war again break out with its center upon the Pacific Ocean, but sweeping and encircling the whole globe.

I saw that the opposing forces were roughly divided by so-called *Christianity* on the one side, and by the so-called followers of *Mohammed* and *Buddha* upon the other. I saw that the great driving power within these so-called Christian Nations, was the *Great Apostasy of Rome, in all its political, social and religious aspects*. I saw the world wide dislocation and devastation of production and slaughter of people occur more swiftly and upon a larger scale than ever before. *I saw an antagonism begin to express itself from those so-called Christian nations against your people.* I saw those of a similar faith to yours in the far east begin to look toward Palestine for safety.

I saw the *international world war* automatically break down, and national revolutions occur in every country, and complete the work of chaos and desolation. I saw geological disturbances occur, which helped in this work as if it were intended to do so. I saw the Cardston temple preserved from all of this geological upheaval. I saw the international boundary line disappear as these two governments broke up and dissolved into chaos. *I saw race rioting upon the American continent on a vast scale.*

Hunger and Disease to Afflict America

I saw *hunger and starvation* in this world granary of the American continent sweep off vast numbers of those conflicting elements. I saw disease produced by hunger, strife and chaos complete the end of this present order or epoch. How long these events were in reaching this consummation, I do not know, but my impression was from the outbreak of the international war these things developed in a continuous procession, and almost ran concurrently, as it is with a sickness, the various symptoms are all in evidence at one and the same time, but in different stages of development.

My intensified thought was, "What of the Church, if such is to become the Kingdom of the earth?" The thought was immediately answered by a subconscious statement. "As it is in the church today," and I saw these higher spiritual beings throughout the length and breadth of the air, marshalling their spiritual forces, and concentrating them upon the high officials of your church upon earth.

I saw the spiritual forces working upon those officers, impressing and moving them, influencing and warning them. I saw the spiritual forces begin to unfold these things into the minds of your elders and other high officials, especially during their spiritual devotions and official duties, and those activities which exalt the mind of the individual or groups. I saw the impressions take hold and inspire the more receptive and spiritual men, until it was all clearly revealed to them in the way the spiritual patriarchs desired.

Divine Guidance Given to Church Leaders

Again I seemed to hear the words, *"As it will be." I saw the high officials in council, and under inspired guidance issue instructions to your people, to reconsecrate their lives and energies to their faith*, to voluntarily discipline themselves, by abstaining from all those forms of indulgence which weaken the body, sap the mentality, and deaden the spirit or waste their income.

I saw further on, instructions given whereby *places of refuge* were prepared quietly but efficiently by inspired elders. I saw Cardston and the surrounding foothills, especially north and west, for miles, being prepared as a refuge for your people quietly but quickly.

I saw artesian wells and other wells dug all over that territory so that when the open waters were polluted and poisoned that the people of the church and their cattle should be provided for. I saw the fuel resources of the district develop in many places and vast piles of coal and timber stored for future use and building.

I saw elders *still under divine guidance*, counseling and encouraging the planting of every available acre of soil in this district, so that large supplies would be near the refuge. I saw the church property under cultivation of an intensified character, not for sale or profit, but for the use of the people. I saw the inspired officers giving instructions as to what would be the best crops to plant and cultivate, not for profit but for use in storage at the time of chaos. I saw the territory carefully surveyed and mapped out, for the camping of a great body of the people of the church. I saw provision also made for a big influx of people who will not at first belong to the church, but who will gather in their tribulation. I saw vast quantities of *surgical appliances, medicines, disinfectants, etc.,* stored in the Temple basement. I saw inspiration given the elders whereby the quantity, quality, and kind of things to be stored were judged, which might not be attainable in this territory in time of chaos. *I saw defensive preparations made and stored as suggested by the power of inspiration.* I saw the elders working out the organizations of the camps upon maps. I saw the mining corridors used as places of storage underground; I saw the hills surveyed and corrals built in sequestered places for cattle, sheep, etc., quietly and quickly. I saw the plans for the organization of the single men and their duties, the scouts, the guards, the nurses, the cooks, the messengers, the children, the herders, the temple guards, etc. I saw all these preparations going on practically unknown to the Gentile world, except to the Great Apostasy, whose knowledge and hatred is far reaching, in this day of its temporary power. This was going on piece by piece as the Elders were instructed so to do.

I saw the other officials obeying the inspired instructions, carrying their message and exhorting the people to carry out from time to time the revelations given them, whilst all around throughout the Gentile world the chaos developed in its varying stages, faction against faction, nation against nation, but all in open or secret hostility to your people and their faith. I saw your people draw closer and closer together, as this became more intense and as the spiritual forces warned them through the mouth of your elders and your other officers. I saw the spiritual forces influencing those members who had drifted away, to re-enter the fold. I saw a greater tithing than ever before. I saw vast quantities of necessaries *supplied by members*

whose spiritual eyes had been opened. I saw a liquidation
of properties and effects disposed of quietly but quickly by
members of the church, as the spiritual influences directed them.

The Saints Instructed to Gather to the Refuges of Zion

I saw the inspired call sent forth to all the church, to
gather to the refuges of Zion. I saw the stream of your people quietly moving in the direction of their refuge. I saw
your people moving more quickly and in larger numbers
until all the stragglers were housed. I saw the wireless
messages flashed from Zion's refuge to Zion's refuge in
their several places, that all was well with them, and then
the darkness of chaos closed around the boundaries of
your people, and the last days of tribulations had begun.[6]

---

[6] As quoted by Duane S. Crowther in *Inspired Prophetic Warnings*, pp.
196-201. See also Robert W. Smith and Elizabeth A. Smith, *The Last
Days*, pp. 44-54 (emphasis added).

Indian Prophets
Speak of the Latter Days

Native Americans or American Indians from all over the Western Hemisphere have met and compared their sacred religious traditions. A great many of their prophecies and traditions are very similar, particularly those concerning a great destruction or day of purification that is going to cleanse America and the world before the second coming of the great white god. The following is but a sampling of one of them.

Native American Prophecies from Central America

The following account is taken from the book, *The Great White Chief, Echa Tah Echa Nah, The Mighty and Wise One*, by Norman C. Pierce. It is an account of two brother explorers and archaeologists of American Indian blood known only as "Paul and I" and their travels among the Natives of South and Central America. Pierce states that the events mentioned in this account seem to have taken place during a three-year period in the mid-thirties. It takes place somewhere close to the Guatemala-Yucatan border and documents these brothers' explorations and experiences among the white Indians that reside there. It was during these visits that they first heard mention of a "*Golden Library*" that is purported to be records containing "all the history of the world from the beginning of time up to the present day, and also into the future."[1] These

---

[1] Norman C. Pierce, *The Great White Chief, Echa Tah Echa Nah, The Mighty and Wise One*, p. 25.

records were in the possession of an Indian people known as the Tzichallas, whose leader was known as Itzla Chelan. Itzla Chelan and his tribe were located somewhere in the Yucatan. After extracting a vow from the two brother explorers to never divulge all of the information to anyone concerning this vast library, Itzla Chelan began to freely talk about many of the things that were written in this great golden archive of world history.

Itzla Chelan Speaks of a Sacred Golden Library of Books

Paul and I were very much interested when he told us that the vast library had been brought to the Western World from the Old World. These records contained all the history of the old world from the beginning up to the time the records were brought to the New World. From that time hence, a record of all important events has been added as they occurred up to the present time. These books contain all the data and history of Peru, Ecuador, Columbia and some parts of Brazil. From what he described to us, we were under the impression that there was also a story pertaining to Central America, their advancement and progress up to the time of the Spanish invasion.

What information we received from Itzla Chelan indicated that these records were in possession of the Inca people at one time. During the time of the Spanish invasion, they were smuggled out of Peru prior to the fall of the Inca civilization. For some time the records were in Peru, also in Colombia, but they were guarded with the utmost secrecy and kept on a continual move, always ahead of the Spanish Conquistadores. They were brought up into Central America, and at one time were in the care of the Maya, and later on were in [the] care of the Toltecs, finally coming into possession of the Aztecs.

During the time of Cortez's invasion, they were smuggled out of what is now Mexico City, taken by day and by night by a group who vowed to always see that these records were safely kept, and to guard them with their lives. About the time of the fall of the Aztec nation, they were taken to a place of secrecy, known only to but a very choice few, where they have been hidden and guarded, and where they are now located. The exact hiding place of this priceless library is known to only a handful of the highest and most elect leaders of the Indian people of the Western Hemisphere.[2]

At this point the brothers were sworn again to absolute secrecy by Itzla Chelan. He then bestowed upon them the great honor and privilege of allowing them to see one of the books from the Golden Library. For five hours the brothers were blindfolded and taken through what seemed to be an endless chain of high mountains, low valleys, mushy swamplands and desert lands. Finally they were informed that they had reached the end of their journey. They were then assisted into a sitting position and then their blindfolds were removed. As their vision cleared, Itzla Chelan motioned them to follow him. They traveled a short distance through heavy jungle growth to a small clearing. Within the clearing they could see an altar-like pedestal covered with a white blanket upon which lay, unopened, one of the books from the Golden Library. They then were allowed to examine the book in great detail. This they did with great respect:

> The top and bottom covers of the book were of a white marble-like stone about a quarter of an inch thick. These pieces of stone measured about ten inches long. Between these two thin slabs of stone were the leaves, which were about nine and one-half inches wide and thirteen inches in length. The leaves of this book were composed of metal, which Paul and I took to be brass or copper of a very light hue.
>
> As we lifted the book we knew immediately by its weight that its leaves were not made of gold. These leaves were about the thickness of three or four sheets of ordinary

---

[2] *Ibid.*, pp. 25-26.

bond typing paper. The book was held together by three small metal rings spaced equally apart at the back of the book. At the center top, and center bottom, as well as center front, were placed additional rings like those in the back of the book, holding it closed together.

We were permitted to open the book and examine its contents. By unlocking and lifting out the rings in the center front, top and bottom, the exquisitely polished stone cover was turned back, exposing the very finely hammered metal plates. Delicately chiseled into the metal sheets were characters which Paul and I, during any part of our career, had never seen anything exactly like it.

. . . When asked if there were any other books that resembled this one, he very readily answered that there are many others from whence this one came; many of them larger, but none smaller than this one. There are many different tongues that are used in the remaining ones. Wishing to press him no further, we refrained from questioning him about the others, for we were highly elated over being privileged to see this one book.[3]

The Words of Echa Tah Echa Nah

Echa Tah Echa Nah (*The Mighty and Wise One*), the Great White Chief of the Chigaraguan people, was visited by the brothers in 1936 and had reached the advanced age of 90 at that time. He was about six feet three inches tall and weighed approximately two hundred and thirty pounds. His hair was snow white and very abundant. His face could show calmness and serenity and yet be very stern, firm and hard. His eyes were his most commanding feature. They would change color from dark blue to black, brown or hazel, depending upon the depth of emotion he felt about whatever subject was being discussed. He carried himself in a very majestic straight and erect manner, always moving very gracefully. It was at once very apparent to the brothers that he was a man of divine inspiration

---

[3] *Ibid.*, pp. 29-30.

and wisdom and they could easily understand why all Indian people held him in such great reverence.

The brothers were amazed to learn that he had a vast knowledge of numerous ancient languages. He had the ability to translate fluently and at random any one of many long-dead dialects found in the enormous library of ancient records in his charge (a different library of records than the one in the previous account). These records were kept in a small room, adjoining their sacred Temple, that had been set aside to keep both sacred and historical records. Some of these records were written on parchment and skins and there were some that were written on metal plates. Many were written in hieroglyphics, pictographs, and petroglyphs. They were also recorded in various other ancient languages and dated back prior to 480 B.C. Echa Tah Echa Nah could translate any of these ancient manu-scripts from which he was reading into the Aztecaza tongue. He also spoke many modern languages. Echa Tah Echa Nah talked with the brothers about many things and he spoke at length about the great events of the past and many events that were far into the distant future.

Paul was eventually adopted by Echa Tah Echa Nah as his son, through the blood ritual. After the adoption, the explorers were privileged to visit the great library where Echa Tah Echa Nah would read to them of the many catas-trophes that had come to pass not only on the Western hemisphere but all the world as well. He also read of many things that were to transpire in the future. The great leader explained to them that he was the 32nd Echa Tah Echa Nah (*The Mighty and Wise One*) since the first one. This title has passed from father to son in true patriarchal order since that time.

Echa Tah Echa Nah
Speaks of a Great Temple to Be Built

He prophesied of the time to come when a Great Tem-ple or *Kiva* would be built at some distant place by the Indian people *and by others* who believe in all the laws and commandments which the Messiah left with them in the beginning; but this would not be until after the cleansing of the earth.[4]

The Day of Purification

The cleansing process was described as a mammoth catastrophe or holocaust that would engulf the earth, ridding it of all evil forces, and only those who believed in and abided by these laws would survive. Then, after the earth would cease to shake and the storms subsided, the survivors would go forth and bury the dead, and also care for the sick and wounded.

. . . This is the day that the faithful will be forewarned to take refuge in caves and tunnels until this indignation of the Lord be overpast.[5]

Preparations Made for the Great Trek North

After the dead have been buried and the injured have recovered, Echa Tah Echa Nah will send a message to all the survivors of the great catastrophe and give them instructions to begin to prepare for the great journey to the North. Echa Tah Echa Nah will then send messengers to Chi Chi Suma, *who is second in command*, directing him to also call all the survivors in his area of the country and have them begin to prepare also for the great trek.

These preparations will begin many months in advance of the actual journey back. This will be necessary as it will require a great amount of foodstuffs and other necessities to survive the pilgrimage back to the North country.

The people are now watching and waiting for this future period to arrive. When the time comes to begin these preparations they will follow the instructions that they have been given by Echa Tah Echa Nah and prepare all needful things for the great trek back.

---

[4] *Ibid.*, p. 80 (emphasis added).
[5] *Ibid.*, p. 81.

Temple Stones Prepared

The brothers also speak of preparations being made by the Indians to furnish materials for the adornment and beautification of a great temple:

> During this period of waiting, the people are not idle for they have hand-hewn and polished all the stone blocks to be used in the Great Temple, and hand polished the white mountain mahogany wood that will be used to beautify this most sacred edifice.
>
> Each stone is cut so that it will be interlocked to the stone adjoining it. Dumbbell-like keystones link them together. No nails will be used in the building of this unique structure. All woodwork will be fitted together with wooden pegs or pins. Only the most precious metals will be used for decorative purposes. However, these will have no face value during this period for *there will be no medium of exchange.* Semi-precious stones such as jasper, turquoise, sardonix, lapis lazuli, and amethyst will be used to add splendor to the interior of this Most Holy Temple.
>
> . . . After the disasters, two great people will leave the Chigaraguan country forever to begin their trek to the site where this Great Temple is to be erected. *Following divine guidance and inspiration,* the place will not be difficult to locate. There they will make preparations and begin work on the Holy Temple, and the Holy City within walls.[6]

The gigantic responsibility of moving the stones for the Great Temple will be one of the last important feats of preparation before the move. These immense stones have already been prepared and stored in the quarries from which they were cut. Due to the enormous weight of these great stones it will be necessary to exercise great care in order to protect the finish that has been given them. These massive stones will be transported by crude means to the

---

[6] *Ibid.,* pp. 82-83 (emphasis added).

shore line, where mammoth barges will have been assembled to carry them to their destination.

Each party will consist of a forward vanguard, that will be followed by the livestock, pack horses and carts, the women and children will be next, traveling beside the rear guard. *All forms of modernization will have been done away with. The devastation and destruction brought about by great disaster will leave only the most primitive form of travel.*

The second party led by Chi Chi Suma will continuously search for a great, white, flat stone located somewhere on the west side of the river. When they find this white stone they will know that they have arrived at their final destination.

After an unspecified period of time and a great deal of travel and searching for this stone, the advance scouts will report that they have located it. Chi Chi Suma will then know that they have reached the end of their journey. He and his councilmen will then draw up the plans necessary to begin the preparations for the building of the Holy Temple and city within a wall. The great stones for the temple will then be unloaded and the great responsibility of building the temple will soon be fully underway.

Immediately after Chi Chi Suma and his group leave, along with the barges for the East, Echa Tah Echa Nah will take his group toward the West. The advance scouts of Echa Tah Echa Nah will be instructed to look for a low range of mountains that run from north to south. After many days of travel toward the West, the scouts will report that they have found the mountain range that they were in search of. When the rest of the party arrives at this low mountain range they will set up camp and rest for a few days before making the necessary preparations to continue their journey to the North. The explorer brothers were told that other survivors of the great disaster would be found who would seek to join the party of Echa Tah Echa Nah.

Other Survivors of the Great Holocaust Are Found

After the people and animals have rested, they will follow this range of mountains to the North, keeping on the east side of this range at all times. As this group slowly travels to the North, *other survivors of this great holocaust of destruction, will timidly seek to join with the Chigaraguan people on their great trek.*

These survivors will not be able to understand the words of the Chigaraguans, nor the Chigaraguans understand the words of the survivors, *yet each will recognize the other by their marks, signs and symbols.* The Chigaraguans will welcome the survivors to join them on their trek. As they advance slowly to the North, almost daily other survivors will join them.

Echa Tah Echa Nah's advance scouts will be on the lookout for a *great stone marker not far from a vast area surrounded by a very white substance. This substance will surround a tremendous inland body of water.* Yet, at all times Echa Tah Echa Nah's group shall stay on the east side of the range of mountains.

Soon his scouts will report the finding of *the great stone marker, and upon arriving at this marker will remain there for many days.* During their stay at this marker, Echa Tah Echa Nah's group will be joined by *another people from the North.*

. . . Many of the survivors, who will have joined the two groups *will have very fair skin and very blond hair,* others will be Indian people, but all will have the same purpose in view as the groups of Echa Tah Echa Nah and Chi Chi Suma—that of taking part in the building of this magnificent edifice of worship to their God—*the Temple of His Coming!*

As the construction of this Most Holy Temple continues, the people who are taking part in its construction are happy in their daily tasks,—and nighttime slowly descends upon the day after tomorrow.[7]

---

[7] *Ibid.*, pp. 81-89 (emphasis added).

The foregoing accounts of our Lamanite brethren and their participation in the building of a great temple is in perfect harmony with the teachings of The Church of Jesus Christ of Latter-day Saints. We believe that a great temple will be built in America in Jackson County, Missouri by a remnant of the house of Jacob "and also as many of the house of Israel as shall come" (3 Nephi 21:23).

Who Will Build the Temple?

As previously mentioned, Wilford Woodruff recorded in his journal entry of December 16, 1877 that he "saw people coming from the river and different places a long way off to help build the Temple."[8] This statement is very broad in scope and could quite possibly not only refer to the return of the Lost Ten Tribes from the north but also to the other remnant survivors of the great holocaust as well.

There has been some confusion within the church implying that the Lamanites would take the lead in building the temple in the New Jerusalem. President Joseph Fielding Smith tells us that the 20th and 21st Chapters of Third Nephi are the main cause of this misunderstanding and misinterpretation. President Smith explains:

> In these chapters the Lord is speaking throughout of *the remnant of Jacob*. Who is Jacob whose remnant is to perform this great work in the last days? Most assuredly *Jacob is Israel*. Then again, when he speaks of the seed of Joseph, who is meant? Those who are descendants of Joseph, son of Israel, and this includes, of course, the Lamanites as well as the *Ephraimites* who are now being assembled and who are taking their place, according to prophecy, at the *head to guide and bless the whole house of Israel* (D&C 133:30; Genesis 48:15-20; Deuteronomy 33:13-17).
>
> . . . I take it we, the members of the Church, most of us of the tribe of Ephraim, are of the remnant of Jacob. *We*

---

8   Susan Staker, Editor, *Waiting For World's End, The Diaries of Wilford Woodruff*, p. 322-325.

know it to be the fact that the Lord called upon the descendants of Ephraim to commence his work in the earth in these last days. We know further that he has said that he set Ephraim, according to the promises of his birthright, at the head. *Ephraim receives the "richer blessings,"* these blessings being those of *presidency or direction. The keys are with Ephraim.* It is Ephraim who is to be endowed with *power to bless* and *give to the other tribes, including the Lamanites, their blessings.* All the other tribes of Jacob, including the Lamanites, are to be crowned with glory in Zion *by the hands of Ephraim.*

Now do the scriptures teach that Ephraim, after doing all of this is to abdicate, or relinquish his place, and give it to the Lamanites and then receive orders from this branch of the "remnant of Jacob" in the building of the New Jerusalem? This certainly is inconsistent with the whole plan and with all that the Lord has revealed in the Doctrine and Covenants in relation to the establishment of Zion and the building of the New Jerusalem.

. . . That the remnants of Joseph, found among the descendants of Lehi, *will* have part in this great work is certainly consistent, and the great work of this restoration, the building of the temple and the City of Zion, or New Jerusalem, will fall to the lot of the descendants of Joseph, but it is *Ephraim who will stand at the head and direct the work* (Ether 13; D&C 133:34, emphasis added).[9]

The lost Ten Tribes of Israel will return from their exile in the north countries to this chosen land to take part in this great temple-building effort preparatory to the second coming of the Savior.

President Spencer W. Kimball stated that "they will return with their prophets, and their sacred records will be a third witness for Christ. They, the Ten Tribes, you, the Lamanites, and the believing of us, also carrying the blood of Israel, will *jointly build the city* to our God, the

---

[9] Bruce R. McConkie, Compiler, *Doctrines of Salvation: Sermons and Writings of Joseph Fielding Smith,* Vol. 2, pp. 248, 250-251.

New Jerusalem, with its magnificent temple."[10] The Lost Ten Tribes will then turn to the children of Ephraim to receive their inheritance. "The Ten Tribes are to be led to Zion, there to receive honor at the hands of those who are of Ephraim, who necessarily are to have previously gathered there. It is plain that Zion is to be first established."[11]

In Doctrine and Covenants 133:26 we learn that the Ten Tribes will be led by "*their prophets.*" Thus we may also safely assume that other groups of righteous survivors may also be led by "their prophets" and inspired leaders such as Echa Tah Echa Nah, and bring back their people and histories also. Reinforcing this belief concerning other "prophets," Elder Orson Pratt had this to say:

"Their Prophets shall hear his voice." (D&C 133:26) Do not think that we are the only people who will have Prophets. God is determined to raise up Prophets among that people, but he will not bestow upon them all the fulness of the blessings of the Priesthood. The fulness will be reserved to be given to them after they come to Zion. But Prophets will be among them while in the north, and a portion of the Priesthood will be there; and John the Revelator will be there, teaching, instructing and preparing them for this great work; for to him were given the keys for the gathering of Israel, at the time when he wrote that little book while on the Isle of Patmos. At that time, John was a very old man; but the Lord told him that he must yet prophesy before many kingdoms, and nations, and peoples, and tongues, and he has got that mission to perform, and in the last days the spirit and power of Elias will attend his administrations among these ten tribes, and he will assist in preparing them to return to this land.[12]

[10] Spencer W. Kimball, *Conference Report*, October 1959, p. 61 (emphasis added).
[11] James E. Talmage, *Articles of Faith*, p. 309.
[12] Orson Pratt, *Journal of Discourses*, Vol. 18, April 11, 1875, pp. 25-26.

The conditions spoken of by Elder Pratt may also apply to other remnant groups as well. In Second Nephi the Lord, speaking to the Gentiles, chastens and rebukes those in this day who would believe that no other nation or people could have their own inspired records:

> Thou fool, that shall say: A Bible, we have got a Bible, and we need no more Bible. . . .
>
> Know ye not that there are more nations than one? Know ye not that I, the Lord your God, have created all men, and that I remember those who are upon the isles of the sea; and that I rule in the heavens above and in the earth beneath; and I bring forth my word unto the children of men, yea, even upon all the nations of the earth?
>
> Wherefore, because that ye have a Bible ye need not suppose that it contains all my words; neither need ye suppose that I have not caused more to be written.
>
> For behold, I shall speak unto the Jews and they shall write it; and I shall also speak unto the Nephites and they shall write it; and I shall also speak unto the other tribes of the house of Israel, which I have led away, and they shall write it; and I shall also speak unto all nations of the earth and they shall write it (2 Nephi 29:6, 7, 10, 12).

The Lord has made it perfectly clear that He has given the directive to keep an account of His words and dealings to many nations and races. All of these forgotten records and testimonies of God will come forth to the children of men in His own due time. And this He does to "prove unto many that I am the same yesterday, today, and forever; and that I speak forth my words according to mine own pleasure" (2 Nephi 29:9).

And it shall come to pass afterward, that I will pour out my spirit upon all flesh; and your sons and your daughters shall prophesy, your old men shall dream dreams, your young men shall see visions:

And also upon the servants and upon the handmaids in those days will I pour out my spirit.

—Joel 2:28-29

7

"A Dream"
The Vision of Charles D. Evans

The following dream was experienced by Patriarch Charles D. Evans and printed in 1894 in *The Contributor* magazine, representing the Young Men's Mutual Improvement Association of The Church of Jesus Christ of Latter-day Saints:

> While I lay pondering, in deep solitude, of the events of the present, my mind was drawn into a reverie such as I had never felt before. A strong solicitude for my imperiled country utterly excluded every other thought and raised my feelings to a point of intensity I did not think it possible to endure. While in this solemn, profound and painful reverie of mind, to my infinite surprise, a light appeared in my room, which seemed to be soft and silvery as that diffused from a northern star. At the moment of its appearance the acute feeling I had experienced instantly yielded to one of calm tranquillity.

A Heavenly Messenger Appears to Give Comfort

> Although it may have been at the hour of midnight and the side of the globe whereon I was situated was excluded from the sunlight, yet all was light and bright and warm as an Italian landscape at noon; but the heat was softer or more subdued. As I gazed upward, I saw descending through my bedroom roof, with a gently gliding movement, a personage clothed in white apparel, whose countenance was smoothly serene, his features regular, and the flashes of his eye seemed to shoot forth scintillations, to use an earthly comparison, strongly resembling those reflected from a diamond under an intensely illumined electric light, which dazzled but did not bewilder. Those large,

deep, inscrutable eyes were presently fixed upon mine, when instantly placing his hands upon my forehead his touch produced an indescribable serenity and calmness, a calmness not born of earth, but at once peaceful, delightful and heavenly. My whole being was imbued with a joy unspeakable. All feelings of sorrow instantly vanished. Those lines and shadows which care and sorrow impress upon us were dispelled as a deep fog before a blazing sun. In the eyes of my heavenly visitor, for such he appeared to me, there was a sort of lofty pity and tenderness infinitely stronger than any such feelings I ever saw manifested in ordinary mortals. His very calm appeared like a vast ocean stillness, at once overpowering to every agitated emotion.

By some intuition, or instinct, I felt he had something to communicate to soothe my sorrows and allay my apprehensions. Whereon, addressing me, he said:

"Son, I perceive thou hast grave anxieties over the perilous state of thy country, that thy soul has felt deep sorrow for its future. I have therefore come to thy relief and to tell thee of the causes that have led to this peril. Hear me attentively. Seventy-one years ago, [1823] after an awful apostasy of centuries, in which all nations were shrouded in spiritual darkness, when the angels had withdrawn themselves, the voice of prophets hushed, and the light of Urim and Thummim shone not, and the vision of the seers was closed, while heaven itself shed not a ray of gladness to lighten a dark world, when Babel ruled and Satan laughed, and church and priesthood had taken their upward flight, and the voice of nations, possessing the books of the Jewish prophets [Bible], had ruled against vision and against Urim, against the further visits of angels, and against the doctrine of a church of apostles and prophets, thou knowest that then appeared a mighty angel [Moroni] with the solemn announcement of the hour of judgment, the burden of whose instructions pointed to dire calamities upon the present generation.[1]

---

[1] See the "*Testimony of the Prophet Joseph Smith*" in the Book of Mormon.

This, therefore, is the cause of what thou seest and the end of the wicked hasteneth."

Prosperity Followed by Lawlessness and Blood

My vision now became extended in a marvelous manner, and the import of the past labors of the Elders was made plain to me. I saw multitudes fleeing *to the place of safety in our mountain heights*. The church was established in the wilderness. Simultaneously the nation had reached an unparalleled prosperity, wealth abounded, new territory was acquired, commerce extended, finance strengthened, confidence was maintained, and peoples abroad pointed to her as the model nation, the ideal of the past realized and perfected, the embodiment of the liberty sung by poets, and sought for by sages.

"But," continued the messenger, "Thou beholdest a change. Confidence is lost. Wealth is arrayed against labor, labor against wealth, yet the land abounds with plenty for food and raiment, and silver and gold are in abundance. Thou seest also that letters written by a Jew have wrought great confusion in the finances of the nation which, together with the policy of many wealthy ones, has produced distress and do presage further sorrow."

Factions now sprang up as if by magic; capital had entrenched itself against labor throughout the land; labor was organized against capital. The voice of the wise sought to tranquilize these two powerful factors in vain. Excited multitudes ran wildly about; strikes increased; lawlessness sought the face of regular government. At this juncture I saw a banner floating in the air whereon was written the words Bankruptcy, Famine, Floods, Fire, Cyclones, Blood, Plague. *Mad with rage, men and women rushed upon each other. Blood flowed down the streets of cities like water. The demon of bloody hate had enthroned itself on the citadel of reason; the thirst for blood was intenser than that of the parched tongue for water. Thousands of bodies lay untombed in the streets.* Men and women fell dead from the terror inspired by fear. Rest was but the precursor of the bloody work of the morrow. All around lay the mournfulness of a past in ruins. Monuments erected to perpetuate the names of the noble and brave were ruthlessly destroyed by combustibles. A voice now sounded aloud these words, "Yet once again I shake not the earth only, but also heaven. And this word yet once again signifies the removing of things that are shaken, as of things that are made; that those things that cannot be shaken may remain."

Earthquakes, Missiles and Plagues to Decimate Mankind

Earthquakes rent the earth in vast chasms, which engulfed multitudes; terrible groaning and wailings filled the air; the shrieks of the suffering were indescribably awful. Water wildly rushed in from the tumultuous ocean whose very roaring under the mad rage of the fierce cyclone, was unendurable to the ear. Cities were swept away in an instant, *missiles were hurled through the atmosphere at a terrible velocity and people were carried upward only to descend an unrecognized mass.* Islands appeared where ocean waves once tossed the gigantic steamer. In other parts voluminous flames, emanating from vast fires, rolled with fearful velocity destroying life and property in their destructive course. The seal of the dread menace of despair was stamped on every human visage; men fell exhausted, appalled and trembling. Every element of agitated nature seemed a demon of wrathful fury. Dense clouds, blacker than midnight darkness, whose thunders reverberated with intonations which shook the earth, obscured the sunlight. Darkness reigned, unrivaled and supreme.

Again the light shone, revealing an atmosphere tinged with a leaden hue, which was the precursor of an unparalleled plague whose first symptoms were recognized by a purple spot which appeared on the cheek, or on the back of the hand, and which, invariably, enlarged until it spread over the entire surface of the body, producing certain death. Mothers, on sight of it, cast away their children as if they were poisonous reptiles. This plague, in grown persons, rotted the eyes in their sockets and consumed the tongue *as would a powerful acid or an intense heat.* Wicked men, suffering under its writhing agonies, cursed God and died, as they stood on their feet, and the birds of prey feasted on their carcasses.

I saw in my dream the messenger again appear with a vial in his right hand, who addressing me said: "Thou knowest somewhat of the chemistry taught in the schools of human learning, behold now a chemistry sufficiently powerful to change the waters of the sea."

He then poured out his vial upon the sea and it became putrid as the blood of a dead man, and every living soul therein died. Other plagues followed I forbear to record.

A foreign power had invaded the nation which, from every human indication, it appeared would seize the government and supplant it with monarchy. I stood trembling at the aspect, when, lo, *a power arose in the west which declared itself in favor of the constitution in its original form;* to this suddenly rising power every lover of constitutional rights and liberties throughout the nation gave hearty support. The struggle was fiercely contested, *but the stars and stripes floated in the breeze, and bidding defiance to all opposition, waved proudly over the land.* Among the many banners I saw, was one inscribed thus: "The government based on the Constitution, now and forever;" on another, "Liberty of Conscience, social, religious and political."

Beautiful Cities with
Eternal Knowledge Fill the Earth

The light of the gospel which had but dimly shone because of abomination, now burst forth with a lustre that filled the earth. Cities appeared in every direction, one of which, in the center of the continent, was an embodiment of architectural science after the pattern of eternal perfections, whose towers glittered with a radiance emanating from the sparkling of emeralds, rubies, diamonds and other precious stones set in a canopy of gold and so elaborately and skillfully arranged as to shed forth a brilliancy which dazzled and enchanted the eye, excited admiration and developed a taste for the beautiful, beyond anything man had ever conceived. Fountains of crystal water shot upward their transparent jets which in the brilliant sunshine, formed ten thousand rainbow tints at once delightful to the eye. Gardens, the perfections of whose arrangement confound all our present attempts at genius, were bedecked with flowers of varied hue to develop and refine the taste, and strengthen a love for these nature's chastest adornments. Schools and universities were erected, to which all had access; in the latter Urims were placed, for the study of the past, present and future, and for obtaining a knowledge of the heavenly bodies, and of the constructions of worlds and universes. The inherent properties of matter, its arrangements, laws, mutual relations were revealed and taught and made plain as the primer lesson of a child. The conflicting theories of geologists regarding the formation and age of the earth were settled forever. All learning was based on eternal certainty. Angels brought forth the treasures of knowledge which had lain hid in the womb of the dumb and distant past.

The appliances for making learning easy surpass all conjecture. Chemistry was rendered extremely simple, by the power which the Urims conferred on man of looking into and through the elements of every kind; a stone furnished no more obstruction to human vision than the air itself. Not only were the elements and all their changes and transformations plainly understood but the construction, operations, and laws of mind were thus rendered equally plain as those which governed the coarser elements. While looking through the Urim and Thummim I was amazed at a transformation, which even now is to me marvelous beyond description, clearly showing the manner in which particles composing the inorganic kingdom of nature are conducted upward to become a part of organic forms; another astounding revelation was a view clearly shown me of the entire circulation of the blood both in man and animals. After seeing these things and gazing once more upon the beautiful city, the following passage of Scripture sounded in my ears: "Out of Zion, the perfection of beauty, God hath shined." (Psalms 50:2)

On this I awoke to find all a dream.

I have written the foregoing, which is founded on true principle, under the caption of a dream, partly to instruct and partly to check the folly of reading silly novels now so prevalent.

Charles D. Evans
Springville, Utah[2]

---

[2] Charles D. Evans, *The Contributor*, representing the Young Men's Mutual Improvement Associations of the Church of Jesus Christ of Latter-day Saints, Vol. 15, August 1894, pp. 638-641, as cited by Duane S. Crowther in *Inspired Prophetic Warnings*, pp. 191-193 (emphasis added).

It seems strange that with all these historical examples of peoples who were destroyed because of unrepented sin, so many pursue a similar course today, including many in America. Yet the promise has been given to the great nations of the Americas that they shall never fall if they will but serve God.

—Spencer W. Kimball,
The Miracle of Forgiveness, p. 139

8

America Attacked, Demoralized and Refreshed

In this chapter we will now review three short visions from Richard Swanson's 1986 book *Spare Your People!* These three visions are similar in content to a number of points in the vision in the previous chapter.

American Military Planes Fail

The first is by Kay Fowler, a housewife and mother from North Carolina. She points out that America will try to defend herself against the foreign invaders without success.

I've also seen a large city with skyscrapers, and enemy planes were coming in and shelling the city. The buildings were on fire and burning as if bombs had been dropped. I saw the people all in a panic, fleeing the city for safety. I've seen New York City harbor completely destroyed. I watched as every ship rolled over and sank. I've seen military jets trying to land and take off from airstrips, and then crash because untrained and unqualified people were placed in command positions. I've seen a squadron of our American jets flying to the war zone, excited about being in war. On each plane was an American flag. I could hear the pilots talking from the cockpit of each of these planes, boasting how powerful their planes were and how great America is. Then, I saw them crashing into the sides of the mountain. "'Though thou exalt thyself as the eagle, and though thou set thy nest among the stars, thence will I bring thee down, saith the Lord." (Obadiah 1:4) In the same revelation I saw that when all

the men are called off to the war zone all the work is left
to the women in that community.[1]

America Invaded but Victorious

The second vision is by John Jackson, who received a
vision wherein he was shown great explosions in many
cities, a foreign invasion of our country and a divine victory for America.

I was looking down upon the United States as I would
a map. I saw many cities in the United States erupt with a
flash that to me signified great explosions.

At this time . . . the Lord is going to provide, but on the
surface this looks so shaky that I don't want the people to
hear this to get anything other than the Lord will see His
people through this time. But what I saw was that the
flashes were a limited exchanging of bombs. I don't know
whether they were nuclear weapons or not, but *there was
a limited exchange of bombs, and that we had been invaded by Russia: literally and physically invaded by Russia.
And that it will appear through this invasion, because it will
totally catch us by surprise, that we had lost the war. But
God told me and revealed to me that He will supernaturally take charge, and when we have given up hope then He
will come in and rescue this land and we will be victorious.
WE WILL BE VICTORIOUS!* I cannot emphasize that enough. But
at the same time the Lord was preparing me, because during this time it will not be a pretty sight; it will not be fun
and games. The Lord is letting us know that we're going to
go through in the coming years and months some tumultuous times; *that without His help we would perish.* During this time, I didn't see it but I knew in my spirit that
Israel was also being invaded [Ezekiel 38, 39], and I also
knew that Russia had waited to invade us until a time
when two things were happening: *one, they felt we were
near internal collapse; and two, we were nearing a break
where we were starting to catch up with them in military*

---

[1] Richard Swanson, *Spare Your People*, p. 149.

strength and might, and before that was going to take place they were going to strike while they felt they still had the upper hand; but our upper hand is God. And our hearts will be turned toward him during that time.[2]

Glory Cloud

The third vision was related in 1972 by a minister from New Zealand who beheld a glorious, beautiful, radiant white cloud arise to envelope America, pushing back a murky black cloud that was also spreading across and enveloping the nation.

I see a [black] cloud arising on the east coast of the United States, and it is spreading across the northeastern section. This black cloud is arising from a spot (I do not know America) but all I can say is it is in the north and in the east over by the sea. This very black, murky cloud is trying to sweep westward and southward. *I can see in the northwest of America another cloud arising, and this cloud is white.* This cloud, because of its brightness, is shining out many glorious, radiant colors. I see there is a conflict between this black, gray, brown, murky cloud and this beautiful, shining, radiant cloud which is rising up . . . But . . . *the black cloud is being overshadowed . . . by the power of the brightness of [the white] cloud.* And now the cloud from the northwest is moving speedily southwestward and eastward, and from underneath it rain is beginning to fall. The color of this rain is pure white. It is raining, but it looks like snow. . . . Small pools of water are beginning to form on the ground. These pools are also like the color of the cloud—white, radiant and sparkling. Small rivers and streams are beginning to flow from each little lake. . . . The rivers, the lakes and more and more of the land mass of America is being covered by this beautiful sparkling water. . . . And not only is America being covered by this beautiful, white, radiant water, but now I see the vision is

---

[2] *Ibid.*, pp. 196-197 (emphasis added).

going further away and I'm beginning to see many other nations of the world.

For behold there are those in these days who would plot, fight, and scheme against thee, who would endeavor to break down the very structure on which thy nation is built. But I say unto thee that the cloud has already risen; that's the Spirit. And behold the cloud that I shall send is a pure cloud dropping pure rain upon pure hearts. And the rivers which I shall send as a result of the rain that shall fall from the cloud no man shall be able to stop, and no weapon formed against thee shall prosper. For I have purposed in My heart, saith God, to revive and refresh, as never before, this nation, and to make you a blessing unto many nations.[3]

Latter-day Saints believe that in the due course of time all living beings on earth will come to the knowledge of the truth, the gospel of Jesus Christ (beautiful sparkling water) "for the earth shall be full of the knowledge of the Lord, as the waters cover the sea" (Isaiah 11:9; Habakkuk 2:14), and "all things shall be made known unto the children of men". (2 Nephi 30:16; see also 2 Nephi 30;15-18)

---

[3] *Ibid.*, pp. 218-220 (emphasis added).

An American Evangelist's Vision

In 1954 an American evangelist recorded the following vision of destruction within the United States. In view of many technological advances that have taken place since this vision, it becomes much more plausible for these events to be understood and believed. Although the identity of the evangelist has remained anonymous, the vision was incorporated into Dr. Charles Taylor's book *World War III and the Destiny of America*, published in 1979 by Sceptre Books.

The evangelist had gone to the observatories atop the Empire State building on a visit to New York City. Upon reaching the top he began to use a giant telescope to view the surrounding area. He had anticipated seeing all of New York City, New Jersey, Manhattan, the Bronx, and beyond the Hudson River to Westchester in a grand panoramic view. However, the vision of his native land that came before him turned out to be far different than he ever could have anticipated:

As I swung the telescope to the north, suddenly the Spirit of God came upon me in a way that I had never thought of before. Seemingly in the spirit I was entirely caught away. I knew that the telescope itself had nothing to do with the distance which I was suddenly enabled to see, for I seemed to see things far beyond the range of the telescope, even on a bright, clear day. It was simply that God had chosen this time to reveal these things to me, for as I looked through the telescope, it was not Manhattan island that I saw, but a far greater scene.

The U.S.A. Spread Out Like a Map

That which I was looking upon was not Manhattan island. It was all of the North American continent spread out before me as a map is spread upon a table. It was not the East River and Hudson River that I saw on either side, but the Atlantic and Pacific Oceans. And instead of the Statue of Liberty standing there in the bay on her tiny island, I saw her standing far out in the Gulf of Mexico. She was between me and the United States.

[Note: As though he was looking at North America from the northern coast of South America.]

There, clear and distinct, lay all the North American continent, with all its great cities. To the north lay the Great Lakes. Far to the northeast was New York City. I could see Seattle and Portland far to the northwest. Down the West Coast, there was San Francisco and Los Angeles. Closer in the foreground, there lay New Orleans, at the center of the Gulf Coast area. I could see the great towering ranges of the Rocky Mountains, and trace with my eye the Continental Divide. All this and more, I could see spread out before me as a great map upon a table.

The Statue of Liberty to Drink, Fall, and Rise No More

As I looked, suddenly from the sky I saw a giant hand reach down. That gigantic hand was reaching out toward the Statue of Liberty. In a moment her gleaming torch was torn from her hand, and in it instead was placed a cup. And I saw protruding from that cup a giant sword, shining, as if a great light had been turned upon its glistening edge. Never before had I seen such a sharp, glistening, edge. Never before had I seen such a sharp, glistening, dangerous sword. It seemed to threaten all the world. As the great cup was placed in the hand of the Statue of Liberty, I heard these words:

> Thus saith the Lord of hosts . . . Drink ye and be drunken, spue, and fall, and rise no more, because of the sword which I will send.

As I heard these words, l recognized them as a quotation from Jeremiah 25:27.

I was amazed to hear the Statue of Liberty speak out in reply, "*I will not drink.*"

Then, as the voice of thunder, I heard again the voice of the Lord, saying:

"*Thus saith the Lord of hosts, Ye shall certainly drink.*" (Jeremiah 25:28)

Then suddenly the giant hand forced the cup to the lips of the Statue of Liberty, and she became powerless to defend herself. The mighty hand of God forced her to drink every drop of the cup. As she drank the bitter dregs, these were the words that I heard:

"*Should ye be utterly unpunished? Ye shall not be unpunished: for I will call for a sword upon all the inhabitants of the earth, saith the Lord of hosts.*" (Jeremiah 25:29)

When the cup was withdrawn from the lips of the Statue of Liberty, I noticed the sword was missing from the cup, which could mean but one thing. The contents of the cup had been completely consumed! I knew that the sword merely typified war, death, and destruction, which is no doubt on the way.

Then, as one drunken on too much wine, I saw the Statue of Liberty become unsteady on her feet and begin to stagger and to lose her balance. I saw her splashing in the gulf, trying to regain her balance. I saw her stagger again and again, and fall to her knees. As I saw her desperate attempts to regain her balance, and rise to her feet again, my heart was filled with compassion for her struggles. But as she struggled there in the Gulf, once again I heard these words:

Ye shall drink and be drunken, and spue, and fall, and rise no more because of the sword that I shall send among you.

As I watched, I wondered if the Statue of Liberty would ever be able to regain her feet—if she would stand again. And as I watched, it seemed that with all her power she struggled to rise, and finally staggered to her feet again, and stood there swaying drunkenly. I felt sure that any moment she would fall again—possibly never to rise again.

I seemed overwhelmed with desire to reach out my hand to keep her head above water, for I knew that if she ever fell again she would drown there in the gulf.

Black Skeleton-Shaped War Cloud Arises Over the U.S.

Then as I watched, another amazing thing was taking place. Far to the Northwest, just over Alaska; a huge, black cloud was arising. As it rose, it was as black as night. It seemed to be in the shape of a man's head. As it continued to rise, I observed two light spots in the black cloud. It rose further, and a gaping hole appeared. I could see that the black cloud was taking the shape of a skull, for now the huge, gaping mouth was plainly visible. Finally the head was complete. Then the shoulders began to appear, and on either side, long, black arms.

It seemed that what I saw was the entire North American continent, spread out like a map upon a table with this terrible skeleton-formed cloud arising from behind the table. It rose steadily until the form was visible down to the waist. At the waist, the skeleton seemed to bend toward the United States, stretching forth a hand toward the east and one toward the west—one toward New York and one toward Seattle. As the awful form stretched forward, I could see that its entire attention seemed focused upon the United States, overlooking Canada—at least for the time being. As I saw the horrible black cloud in the form of a skeleton bending toward America, bending from the waist over, reaching down toward Chicago and out toward both coasts, I knew its one interest was to destroy the multitudes.

First Target—New York City and Eastern U.S.

As I watched in horror, the great black cloud stopped just above the Great Lake region, and turned its face toward New York City. Then out of the horrible, great gaping mouth began to appear wisps of white vapor which looked like smoke, as a cigarette smoker would blow puffs of smoke from his mouth. These whitish vapors were being blown toward New York City. The smoke began to spread until it covered all the eastern part of the United States.

Second Target—West Coast and Los Angeles

Then the skeleton turned to the West, and out of the horrible mouth and nostrils came another great puff of white smoke. This time it was blown in the direction of the West Coast. In a few minutes, the entire West Coast and the Los Angeles area was covered with its vapors.

Third Target—Central U.S.

Then toward the center came a third great puff. As I watched, St. Louis and Kansas City were enveloped in its white vapors. Then it came toward New Orleans. On they swept until they reached the Statue of Liberty where she stood staggering drunkenly in the blue waters of the Gulf. As the white vapors began to spread around the head of the Statue, she took in but one gasping breath and then began to cough as though to rid her lungs of the horrible vapors she had inhaled. One could tell readily by the painful coughing that those white vapors had seared her lungs.

What were these white vapors? . . . Could they be the horrible nerve gas recently made known to the American public?[1]

Russia has been covertly perfecting new chemical weapons specifically designed to exterminate populations. In March, 1994, the *London Sunday Times* reported that the Russians have a new "superplague powder" which was developed in a secret biological weapons program run by the Russian Defense Ministry that is so powerful that 440 pounds sprayed from an airplane or in air-burst bombs could kill 500,000 people. The newspaper reported that the West has no antidote.[2]

---

[1] Charles R. Taylor, *World War III and the Destiny of America*, pp. 99-103. Also Michael Waller, "Russia's Poisonous Secret," *Readers Digest*, Vol. 145, No. 870, October, 1994, pp. 129-133 (emphasis added).

[2] *London Sunday Times*, March 1994.

People Running for Their Lives

As I looked, I saw people everywhere running; but it seemed none of them ran more than a few paces, and then they fell. . . . I now saw millions of people falling in the streets, on the sidewalks, struggling. I heard their screams for mercy and help. I heard their horrible coughings, as though their lungs had been seared with fire. I heard the moanings and groanings of the doomed and dying. As I watched, a few finally reached shelters; but only a few ever got to the shelters.

American Interceptors Fail to Stop Rockets from the Sea

Then suddenly I saw from the Atlantic and from the Pacific, *and out of the Gulf, rocket-like objects that seemed to come up like fish leaping out of the water. High into the air they leaped, each heading into a different direction, but every one toward the United States.* On the ground, the sirens screamed louder. Up from the ground I saw similar rockets beginning to ascend. To me, these appeared to be interceptor rockets although they arose from different points all over the United States. *However, none of them seemed to be successful in intercepting the rockets that had risen from the ocean on every side.* These rockets finally reached their maximum height, slowly turned over, and fell back to earth in defeat. Then suddenly, the rockets which had leaped out of the oceans like fish all exploded at once. The explosion was ear-splitting. The next thing which I saw was a huge ball of fire. The only thing I have ever seen which resembled that which I saw in my vision was the picture of the explosion of the H-bomb somewhere in the Pacific some months ago. In my vision, it was so real I seemed to feel a searing heat from it.

As the vision spread before my eyes, and I viewed the widespread desolation brought about by the terrific explosions, I could not help thinking, "While the defenders of our nation have quibbled over what measures of defense to use, and neglected the only true defense, faith and dependence upon the true and living God, that which she has greatly feared has come upon her! How true it has been proven that 'except the Lord keep the city, the watchman waketh but in vain' [Psalms 127:1]."[3]

---

[3] Charles R. Taylor, *World War III and the Destiny of America*, pp. 105-107 (emphasis added).

They come from a far country, from the end of heaven, yea, the Lord, and the weapons of his indignation, to destroy the whole land.

And I will punish the world for evil, and the wicked for their iniquity; I will cause the arrogancy of the proud to cease, and will lay down the haughtiness of the terrible.

—2 Nephi 23:5, 11

10

The Prince Charles Vision

American Christian Evangelist Henry Gruver began receiving visions from the Lord when he was only 13 years of age. He credits his parents with providing him with a proper religious heritage and training at an early age. He says that he was taught prayer in many ways. He was blessed with a praying mother and a father that loved and studied the word of God. Because of their faith in the Lord he grew up going to places where prophecy was taught. Gruver has traveled the world ministering to people and relating his visions of a coming Russian Invasion of America. Gruver said that he had been receiving visions regarding America's destiny since he was 13, but had not told very many people about them until 1986 when he was told by the Lord to share these visions with others and warn them of these coming events. He was told that if he did not do this, their blood would be on his hands. He has been lecturing and warning as many as would listen ever since.

In the following vision of Henry Gruver, America and England are both targets of an invading army. Chemical weapons seem to be one of the primary implements used in the war.

In this vision, Gruver was led down into the bottom of a canyon along with his wife and children. As they reached the bottom there was a clearing and in the clearing were a General and a U.S. Senator waiting for him by a speaker's platform with chairs. He was welcomed and subsequently introduced to them. As he was waiting he heard a big helicopter fly over the canyon wall. As he looked closer he could see that it was a big double-bladed one, like what the military calls "egg-beaters." It was carrying what looked like a blue construction office. He felt that it had a significant relationship to the United Nations as its color was what he described as United Nations blue.

The construction office was set down and Prince Charles stepped out of it. As the Prince came down the grade and got closer, Gruver began to realize that his face was all red and puffy, his eyes were red as though he had been crying. Prince Charles looked at him and said: *"I thank you for coming today. You're the family I've heard about and you're here at my request. I have a message for you. Please take heed. I must inform you that your nation is at war and you have a battle to fight, but the saddest thing is, you must fight it without God."*

With that the General who had been sitting behind him, an American Four Star General, jumped to his feet and came down off the platform, came around on the ground in front of him and looked at Charles very sarcastically. He said, *"We know we're at war and we know we have a battle to fight but we didn't know God had anything to do with it."*

With that, Charles brought his right hand up and he came right down between the eyes of the General and he said "And sir, that is your mistake."

The Prince and the General then began to argue about why God did or did not have anything to do with it.

Shortly thereafter Gruver was caught up into the heavens looking down on Trafalgar Square, in London. The following is his account:

> Trafalgar Square is one of the largest squares other than Red Square in Moscow. It's a massive square, which has giant lions on the 4 corners of it facing North, South, East and West. The lions themselves are up probably 10 or 12 feet high just to their backs, let alone their heads and are made of brass.

. . . Well the lions were not in the square. The big fountain that you could easily put 3 or 4 of this building into was not there. Nelson's Column was not there in it. The square was empty except for all of the buildings around it and the buildings around it were like commerce, libraries, churches, and government offices. That's the reason I think of Trafalgar Square is because it is a representation of the British Empire in its glory. So it is a representation of everything that you would do to run the empire.

And I'm looking on this square that's empty. There's no statues on it now. And all of the sudden people start running out into this open square from all of these buildings. And they're all dressed in their occupational garb. You can tell their occupation by the apparel that they're wearing.

. . . And as I am in the heavens looking down on this square I didn't see anything but the square at first. The people begin pointing off to my left hand. . . . They're pointing in the direction of my left hand and they're mocking and scoffing and jeering and saying *"You can't hurt us. You don't have any power any more. We're not afraid of you."* And they're literally mocking and I turned to look to see what they are pointing at because they're pointing straight ahead, they're pointing way up and I look. And then my eyes see this army that went from the bottom, right by the square, all the way into the heavens, clear up to the same level I was in, in the heavens.

Off to my left hand was a Russian general fully dressed in his full general's outfit with all of his braid and everything. And I want to say to you that I've been watching for that general to come on the world scene in Russia. He's been hidden up until the Yeltsin Cabinet began to run for office last year and he was going to run against Yeltsin and his name was Lebed. And I was surprised to find out that he is one of the top generals in Russia and he is a military man and still has the military with him.

. . . But here is this general and he is standing in the heavens. *His fists were clenched.* They were down at his side, his chest was out and he was looking down into the square at these people. At his right hand was a rectangular war weapon. To me it looked kind of like an anti-aircraft type multiple cylindered weapon that they'd have on ships, but it wasn't quite. And as this band of people down in the square are mocking his army and are literally scoffing and laughing at them and saying *"You don't have any power. We are not afraid of you."* I saw all of the sudden his neck muscles begin to thicken and his face begin to get a look of tension and he was getting angry and then his blood vessels began to bulge as all of the sudden his fists came up and he said *"Present arms! Aim! Fire!"*

Russian Soldiers
Use Chemical Weapons Against England

And this massive army of footmen that came from the heavens clear down into the level that these people were in, in the square, stood with clenched fists in front of them holding their rifles before he gave the orders to fire. *They were in full chemical warfare gear.* They were firing on the people in this square. As they fired the first shot on these people, I saw something that I believe we're being prepared for today. It totally caught these people by surprise. They sincerely, with their whole heart, did not believe that this massive military had any power and they did not believe that this military would ever fire on them. Because of the response that was taking place there as they were fired on I could see that they were caught by total surprise and total panic. And the whole action of that group of people in that square told me it was a surprise to them even though they knew the army existed. They could see it going into the heavens but they sincerely believed that it would not fire on them.

Gruver had not known that the uniforms that he had seen the Russians wearing were chemical warfare protective clothing until he talked to a man that had come back from maneuvers in Afghanistan. This is what he was told:

> *"Henry, you have perfectly described the Russian chemical warfare uniform."* He said, *"I didn't even know they*

*had that kind of uniform until I just went over there myself
and saw it. We didn't even have pictures to train for these
because they're brand new uniforms. It's the latest of gear
they have. But,"* he said, *"I want to tell you something, your
description of their chest looking like the ribbed look of a
locust of the desert, that was what their chest looked like.
Their face looks almost like a horse in a way, the snoot
somewhat like a horse, and they had big googy eyes."* He
explained to me "the big googy eyes are the goggles. The
head covering they put over them has the goggles and the
snooty look like a horse" he said, and he asked me the colors and everything. "That's exactly what the chemical warfare gear looks like. It has a pre-filtration system and a
breathing apparatus that goes back down into this rib-
looking chest that has multiple filtration systems." And he
said, "that is the most advanced chemical warfare gear
that you can get on the face of the earth. I want to tell you
something, we didn't have anything to match it. They fired
chemicals across and some of my men got into those
chemicals and their chemical warfare gear began to just
melt right off of them." He said, "I don't know what kind of
material they have but we'd better find out. From that
time," he said, "I was scared to death over there. One blast
of this vapor could wipe out my whole platoon."[1]

Aleksandr Ivanovich Lebed

The former Russian general spoken of by Gruver in his
vision, Aleksandr Ivanovich Lebed (pronounced LYEH-
bed), was born in the Russian Cossack town of Novo-
cherkassk. He has been described as a gruff brutal man
who never loses his cool, an outspoken loner, a man willing to rise to any challenge. "Lebed has appeared wherever Russians were fighting and dying: Afghanistan, Baku,
Tbilisi, Moldova. With distinction and frequent acts of
heroism he commanded a battalion in Afghanistan in

---

[1] Henry Gruver, (Video tape presentation of) *Russian Invasion of America*, Virtue International.

1981."[2] Lebed was thrust into the limelight and fame in August of 1991 when under his leadership, a group of tanks defended Yeltsin's White House during the attempted Communist coup. He is "now rated the country's most popular politician, with [popular] support, nearly double Yeltsin's."[3] Lebed has been named by Russian soldiers as "the most popular man in Russia's demoralized army."[4] and has flatly stated that he will become the next president of Russia. He projects a strong image to the people, one of a person who is capable of restoring order.

Lebed's ideology for Russia is centered on her restoration as a great power in the world and he has openly stated that "there will be a new union, whether the West likes it or not."[5]

Lebed is neither shy nor subtle in his comments, often causing quite a stir such as when he verbally attacked Mormons in 1996 by calling them "mold and filth"[6] and that he would prohibit them from doing missionary work in Russia.

In May of 1998 Lebed received a huge boost to his Russian presidential hopes when voters in Siberia elected him Governor of Krasnoyarsk with an impressive 57% of the votes. Lebed has made no secret of his presidential ambitions and this win has propelled him into the top ranks of prospective candidates for Russia's 2000 presidential campaign. This man definitely deserves our

---

[2] Michael Specter, "The Wars of Aleksandr Ivanovich Lebed," *The New York Times Magazine*, October 13, 1996, p. 47.

[3] A. Patricia Kranz, "What's Bringing Moscow Together: Fear of Lebed," *Business Week*, February 10, 1997, p. 59.

[4] *Op. Cit.*, p. 74.

[5] Alan Cooperman, "'There will be a new union,'" *U.S. News and World Report*, October 9, 1995, p. 60.

[6] Lee Davidson, "Lebed Says Criticizing LDS a Mistake," *Deseret News*, http://www.desnews.com/cit/t90mngs4.htm, March 20, 1998.

close attention as he continues his ascent to power within Russia.[7]

The future of Yeltsin's reforms remains clouded as the leadership in the former Soviet Union continues to change and polarize against the West. We would do well to do everything in our power to become informed of Russia's part in the great latter-day drama. We need to be aware of the powerful forces that appear to be leading up to World War III. The Lord does not want his children to be destroyed and taken by total surprise by these evil forces, although it appears the great majority will be. It is our duty to put forth the necessary effort to keep from being deceived. Our own survival may depend on it.

In the following chapter we will reinforce the belief that Russia will yet attack the United States with a similar manifestation received by President George Albert Smith. It also portrays Russia as the principle antagonist in a future attack on the United States.

---

[7] See Associated Press, "Lebed, winning governor's race, sees 'big, difficult' work ahead," *Boston Globe Online*, http://www.boston.com/dailynews/wirehtml/138/Lebed_winning_governor_s_race_see.htm, May 18, 1998.

Surely the Lord God will do nothing, until he revealeth his secret unto his servants the prophets.

Where there is no vision, the people perish:

—*JST* Amos 3:7, Proverbs 29:18

Russia to Attack the United States: A Vision of President George Albert Smith

The following excerpts are from a vision recorded by David Hughes Horne as a witness to his cousin, George Albert Smith's prophetic vision concerning a coming attack on America by Russia. The Prophet said that it was terrible beyond description because of the atomic missiles that would be unleashed against the United States. Brother Horne said that he first heard this prophecy when he was 11 years old, sometime between October, 1946 and January, 1947, when President Smith was invited to speak to the Horne family during a family gathering:

> I have had a troublesome vision of another great and terrible war that made the war just ended [World War II] look like a training exercise, and people died like flies.[1] It began at a time when the Soviet Union's military might dwarfed that of the United States, and we, that is the United States, would have missiles that carried an atomic bomb in Europe. I saw the United States withdraw its missiles to appease the Soviet Union, and then the war began.

Russia to Fire Missiles at American Cities and Military Targets

He also said that we would have big missiles in deep holes he described like grain silos which the Soviets would

---

[1] See George Albert Smith, *Conference Report*, April 1950, p. 169. Also Marion G. Romney, *Conference Report*, April 1968, p. 114.

try to destroy by their own missiles. They would hit military installations and some cities also. He said that the president at that time would be of Greek extraction.

Until then all the presidents would be of British or northern European ancestry. He continued that the U.S. would be bound by numerous entangling alliances and would *take away weapons owned by the people*. He talked some about the initial attack and the ground warfare, but I can't remember enough to document all their tactics and in which countries various things occurred. One tactic, especially in Europe, was to transport tanks in thousands of big trucks like semi-trailers on the super highways to have them located where they wanted them when the war was to begin.

. . . Then he said, "The aftermath was dreadful. Think of the worst, most difficult times of the depression." He turned to us children and said, "You won't remember the depression," which was true. I didn't know there was a depression as I was growing up; the sun came up every morning, flowers bloomed, we went to school, and there was church every Sunday. But he repeated to our parents, "Think of the worst condition of the depression. Can you think of something?" to which our father answered, "Oh Yes!" Then President Smith continued, "You know how Sunday School picnics are complete with salad, chicken, root beer, and dessert, and everyone has a wonderful time. That worst time of the depression will seem like a Sunday School picnic when compared with how conditions will be after that great war." When he finished speaking, he turned around and went to the front door. As he left I thought to myself, "What he said is really important. I've got to remember it!"[2]

Brother Horne then added many of his own comments with regard to how many of our modern technological

---

[2] David Hughes Horne, *A Vision of George Albert Smith*, four page typewritten photocopy in author's possession.

advances have brought us closer to seeing the fulfillment of these predictions in our lifetime:

> When President Smith told us of his vision, the U.S. and the USSR were allies. Some tiffs had occurred between the USSR and the U.S., but the idea that the Soviets would become an enemy wasn't popular. In 1946 the USA was the world's great military power. It seems the allies of the U.S. succeeded in World War II because we had sent them material. The idea that the USSR would dwarf the U.S.'s military might was contrary to any reasonable expectation, but today it is exactly true. The Soviet's military might is awesome. Nearly all their population including peasant farmers serve in their reserves and may become part of their army in time of war. They have amassed a year's supply of food (including U.S. grain) so they will not have to farm the first year of any war. They have about five times as many fighters and several times as many modern bomber aircraft as we do. They are well made, effective aircraft with well trained pilots and crews. Their infantry's weapons and logistics preparations are staggering. Thus, two elements of President Smith's vision were exactly correct; the USSR became our enemy, and their military might dwarfs our own.
>
> . . . It's no secret we have nuclear warhead missiles in Europe and underground silos here. But in 1946 nuclear missiles were beyond imagination. Even [the] Massachusetts Institute of Technology's president in 1950 said. "Intercontinental ballistic missiles with nuclear warheads are impossible." But we had them by 1963; I've worked in Minuteman Missile silos which accurately fit President Smith's description. But our cruise missiles were made after 1980. General Bernard Rogers, NATO Commander, was so outspoken against the INF treaty that he was removed. General John Gains, his successor, said that he could not maintain Europe in a war for more than two weeks without nuclear weapons. So five more elements of President Smith's vision are verified; we have missiles, in

Europe, and in silos, that carry atomic bombs, and are essential for U.S. defense.

Next President Smith said that we would withdraw our missiles from Europe to appease the Soviets. Former UN Ambassador Jean Kirkpatrick said that the INF treaty hurts us militarily, but we have to do it. Dr. Eugene Callens says the treaty was politically motivated, missiles were used as bargaining chips in negotiations with the Soviets, which is a form of appeasement, and Pres. Reagan may have been buying time with their removal until other new systems were in place. During the negotiations we revealed we knew the USSR plans to violate the treaty. Thus two more elements of President Smith's vision are verified: On 1 September, 1983 the U.S. began removing missiles to comply with a treaty designed to appease the Soviets. By December 31,1989 our missiles should be disarmed.

The next elements in President Smith's prophecy were another great and terrible war. It would make World War II look like a training exercise, and people would die like flies. This obviously hasn't happened, but consider some of the Soviets' weapons and military preparations and the results of their use.

Many Soviet Weapons Superior to America's

The Soviets have 100-megaton hydrogen bombs which could be used against military bases and cities. Also, when the Soviets tested one of their first 100-megaton bombs the Electromagnetic Pulse (EMP), which is an incredibly high energy radio wave produced by the detonation, melted an electrical system power transformer's windings 190-miles away. The Soviets are far ahead of the U.S. in space technology and the number of satellites in orbit. From January through September,1987, the Soviets fired more than 700 vehicles into space, mostly military. The U.S. space program for that same time was almost stopped. And some military analysts believe some of the Soviet satellites in orbit above the U.S. contain high yield nuclear bombs purposefully designed to destroy all the transformers in the nation-wide power grid, computers, radios, TVs, telephones and most other electronic devices in the U.S. Pacemakers and electronic watches may be blown out, too. Most transistors, diodes, integrated circuits and other semiconductor devices can tolerate less than 30-volts, but EMP is about a 50,000 volt/meter wave. Evacuation from cities before the bombs hit may be difficult, because new vehicle engines and alternators today have semiconductor controls. Their junction could be melted in a millionth of a second by the EMP. It may be as if for an instant the entire continent were a microwave oven. Older vehicles with points in their distributors and mechanical voltage regulators may continue to operate if their alternator diodes are not blown. Diodes and electronic auto parts can be replaced if spares exist that were shielded. My amateur radio gear with electron tubes still may work afterward. But well pumps that supply our drinking water may be out of service for a long time.

If the war President Smith saw occurs, conditions will be like our pre-1800 ancestors knew with some shelters but few modern machines by which we work. Conditions will be worse for a long time. Government and major services including police, electricity, potable water & waste, fuel and commercial food, medicines, and clothes may not exist. Engines to power pumps, vehicles and machines may not work: Third Nephi 21:14-15 says that if the gentiles don't repent the Lord will destroy their chariots, cities, and strongholds. Our ancestors had wagons and horses for transportation and work. Shovels, hoes, seed, and bikes with puncture-resistant tubes may be scarce. There may be no food from farms other than what will be carried, no manufactured goods, or any safe drinking water. Our forbearers knew how to do things without our machines that we do not know how to do. Thus, conditions could be exactly like President Smith described; the worst conditions of the depression would seem like a Sunday School picnic in comparison.[3]

---

[3] *Ibid* (emphasis added).

War, Calamity and Plague to Engulf the World

It seems that a future period of great destruction, disorder and upheaval is one of the most common denominators throughout the majority of the dreams and visions that we have explored in the previous chapters concerning America. Indian prophet and religious leader Echa Tah Echa Nah described it as a mammoth holocaust that would engulf the whole earth. Four of the visionaries relate in detail various aspects of the destruction. The laws of nature will be in total disarray and earthquakes will rend the earth, engulfing multitudes of people. Water will rush in from the tumultuous ocean and great fires will destroy many lives as well as property.

As in President George Albert Smith's vision, most envisioned a terrible all-encompassing worldwide war yet to come. This great international war will reportedly break out somewhere in the Pacific and continue to expand until it encircles the whole globe. The strength of the United States will be spent conducting war in foreign lands. They saw foreign nations attack the United States with hordes of armed men intent on conquering and dividing up the country. Russia was identified by several as being one of them.

Four of the visionaries watched many cities of the United States being devastated by bombs and missiles. Among those cities specifically referred to were New York City, Boston, Philadelphia, Washington, D.C., Los Angeles, Chicago, Kansas City, St. Louis, and New Orleans. Missouri, Illinois and part of Iowa were to become a complete wilderness. Exploding missiles caused large numbers of people to be carried upward and then descend back down in an unrecognizable mass. Nuclear, biological and chemical warfare could cause unparalleled plagues and loss of life. Millions of people will fall dead in the streets from this attack and lay there un-entombed. Dense clouds will obscure the sunlight. Open waters will become polluted and poisoned, and the sea will become so putrid that everything in it will die.

There will be fear, panic, and race rioting throughout this nation as never before. There will be murders, whoredoms, wickedness and abominations of every kind. Blood will flow in the streets and sheer terror will grip everyone. There will be faction against faction and family against family. Men and women will rush upon each other in deadly rage. Mothers will cut the throats of their own children and eat their raw flesh. Mobocracy will prevail throughout the land. There will be a devastation of food production and the hunger thus caused will produce many diseases. This same horror and destruction will spread over the entire continent. All this will make the depression of the 1930s seem like a Sunday School picnic.

The United States shall be broken up in pieces as a government and its destruction will seem sure. The faithful will be forewarned and places of refuge will be prepared. Multitudes will flee to the mountains to escape the devastation. A power will arise in the west that will proclaim itself in favor of the Constitution in its original form. God will supernaturally rescue this land from conquest and the boys from the mountains will step forth and save a faltering American Army from destruction.

In the following chapter we will analyze Russia, her ambitions to wage war and whether she is currently preparing for a coming war with the United States.

Ours is the dispensation of desolation and war that will be climaxed by a worldwide Armageddon of butchery and blood at the very hour of the coming of the Son of Man. Jesus speaks thus for the elect's sake; none others can read the signs of the times. Carnal men will consider war as a way of life and a norm of society, not as a scourge sent of God to cleanse the earth preparatory to the return of his Son.

—Bruce R. McConkie,
The Mortal Messiah, Vol. 3, p. 441

12

Russia, the Giant of the North, Friend or Foe?

Years ago in the General Conference of April,1966, a prophet of God, President David O. McKay, declared: *"The position of this Church on the subject of Communism has never changed. We consider it the greatest satanical threat to peace, prosperity, and the spread of God's work among men that exists on the face of the earth."*[1]

Years later, in 1989, the Berlin Wall came down and in 1991, newspapers across the world proclaimed the death of the Soviet Union and Communism, and the birth of a new commonwealth. From all outward appearances Communism was in full retreat all across the world. The threat was over. Or was it?

In the early 1930s, Dmitri Z. Manuilski outlined the philosophy of the old hard-line Soviet Communists in a speech at the Lenin School of Political Warfare in Moscow:

> War to the hilt between communism and capitalism is inevitable. Today, of course, we are not strong enough to attack. Our time will come in thirty or forty years. To win, we shall need the element of surprise. The bourgeoisie will have to be put to sleep. *So we shall begin by launching the most spectacular peace movement on record. There will be electrifying overtures and unheard of concessions.* The capitalist countries, stupid and decadent, will rejoice to cooperate in their own destruction. They will leap at another

---

[1] David O. McKay, "Statement on Communism," *The Improvement Era*, Vol. 69, No. 6., June 1966, p. 477 (emphasis added).

chance to be friends. *As soon as their guard is down, we shall smash them with our clenched fist.*[2]

Glasnost and Perestroika Are for Cosmetic Purposes Only

More recently, in November of 1987, it was reported by Sir William Stephenson, who was known as Intrepid and was the head of the Combined Allied Intelligence Operations during WWII, that Mikhail Gorbachev had this to say while speaking to the Politburo of glasnost and perestroika and the coming democratic reform movement within the Soviet Union:

> Gentlemen, comrades, do not be concerned about all you hear about glasnost and perestroika and democracy in the coming years. These are primarily for outward consumption. *There will be no significant internal change within the Soviet Union, other than for cosmetic purposes.*
>
> Our purpose is to disarm the Americans and to let them fall asleep. We want to accomplish three things: *One, we want the Americans to withdraw conventional forces from Europe. Two, we want them to withdraw nuclear forces from Europe. Three, we want the Americans to stop proceeding with [the] Strategic Defense Initiative.*[3]

The Perestroika Deception is the final phase of a strategic communist scheme to bring about the political and physical demise of Western democracies. It refers to the restructuring of not only the Soviet/Russian system, but of the entire free world. KGB agents of influence created a plan to use glasnost or openness to combine accurate information with disinformation and feed it to the West.

---

[2] Dmitri Z. Manuilski, *Lenin School of Political Warfare*, Moscow, 1933 as quoted in *Deceiving America: Communist Influence in the Media*, http://www.inforamp.net/~jwhitley/kgb.htm. Also *League of Prayer*, Volume 1189, November, 1989. p. 3 (emphasis added).

[3] Mikhail Gorbachev, as quoted in "The Gloss of Glasnost 1990," *League of Prayer*, Vol. 1189, November, 1989, p. 3 (emphasis added).

This treacherous ploy of Gorbachev and the Soviet /Russian hierarchy has been accomplished and the so-called "collapse" of Communism, around the world, is nothing more than a continuation of a clever stage production, possum-act strategy that was created to promote the unilateral disarmament of the United States. Hopefully the reader will be able to recognize the obvious parallels with the dreams and visions we have already reviewed.

On April 22, 1990, Vince Ryan, in an interview with retired American diplomat Stephen A. Koczak, over the North America One Satellite Radio Network, discussed the widespread feeling that the former Soviet Union has given up its imperial aims of military victory over the West. Koczak was an American Diplomat who served in West Germany, Hungary and Israel. He has also worked as a consultant to the minority staff of the Senate Foreign Relations Committee.

Based on Koczak's knowledge of the Communist bloc he predicted, a year in advance, that the Berlin Wall would come down—on direct orders of Soviet leader Mikhail Gorbachev. Koczak said the Soviet apparatus has always looked to question how they could increase their power in the world. Under Gorbachev, a strategy that was worked out many years ago was implemented that was designed to do just that:

> The Soviets decided that they would never again wage a war like World War I or World War II.
>
> Any war in the future would be directed *exclusively against the United States and fought on American soil.*
>
> To do that they did not intend to invade the United States. *They would use the submarine system which they were building to launch their missiles to destroy Washington and the American naval bases* and win the war in the first several days.
>
> This way the Soviets would have destroyed the political and military leadership of the United States.

Areas in the center of the United States would not be destroyed.

. . . Gorbachev has had allies first of all in the KGB (*the Soviet secret police*). He is a product of the evolution of the KGB under Yuri Andropov.

Andropov decided after the Hungarian Revolution (*under the sponsorship of then-premier Nikita Khrushchev*) that the KGB had to be transformed from a brutal police force into the most elite, most expert group of strategists, physicists, chemists and politicians in the world.

The members of the KGB became the most expert group in analyzing the United States—not only the president and Congress, but such things as the Trilateral Commission.

. . . The Trilateral Commission was an effort by power brokers within the United States to set up an alliance system—an informal arrangement outside the government itself—between the Japanese, the British and the Americans (*and the French to a certain extent*) to bring in a group of people who control the economics and the finances and the banks to direct the course of world affairs.

. . . Gorbachev's purpose and the KGB's purpose and the military's purpose is to ultimately fight a war against the United States that will be over so fast that the NATO powers will find it meaningless to go to war after the United States is destroyed.

. . . Gorbachev called together his experts and said: "Look, I want to take the initiative and startle these people. I know what they are going to say.

"They are going to complain about the communist governments in Eastern Europe. We'll get rid of them. But before we do it, I want to know how much I need to do in order to get Western investment in the Soviet Union."

His experts told him, "America's high standard of living doesn't arise from the gross national product.

"It comes from one reason alone: While we were building our submarines, the Americans were importing goods and building up a trade deficit."

. . . The Establishment media keeps telling the American people that if Gorbachev accepts the Western model of development that the chance of war is reduced or even eliminated.

. . . But the Soviet Union is now continuing to build submarines and other strategic weapons which, in the event they feel they need to go to war against the United States, they can utilize to win that war, *fought on American Soil.*

. . . This is why Gorbachev had the meetings with Ronald Reagan in Reykjavik, Iceland: to get American nuclear weapons out of Europe.

. . . Now Gorbachev realizes there is no way that the Americans can force the NATO powers to go to war on America's behalf *if Soviet naval forces destroy Washington and America's naval bases.*

. . . They are planning for a war right now, and they will continue to plan for that war.[4]

Similarly, another voice of warning has been raised by Soviet defector Anatoliy Golitsyn. Golitsyn has been sending in-depth analyses and memoranda to CIA and FBI for years warning of the strategic plans the Communists have implemented to conquer the West through deception. He counseled them against believing in the fictional perestroika movement and the so-called democratization within the former Soviet Union. Golitsyn defected to the United States in 1961. He was a member of the Communist Party and served 16 years in the KGB. He is a graduate of the counter-intelligence faculty of the High Intelligence School in Moscow and the University of Marxism-Leninism. He served when the present Soviet strategy of deception was being formulated. He correctly predicted the Communist introduction of economic and political reforms, a false liberation within the USSR and

---

4 Vincent Ryan, "You'll Pay for Gorbachev's Economic and Political Moves," *Spotlight,* interview with Stephen A. Koczak, May 21, 1990, pp. 10-13 (emphasis added).

Eastern Europe. He accurately predicted the legalization of Solidarity in Poland, the return of democratization in Czechoslovakia, and the removal of the Berlin Wall.

Author Mark Riebling carried out a methodical analysis of Golitsyn's 1984 book *New Lies for Old* and its predictions concerning the illusionary changes taking place in the Soviet Union and credited him with an accuracy record of nearly 94%. In his 1998 book *The Perestroika Deception* Golitsyn warned:

> Believers think the Soviet Union is no longer dangerous and that the Cold War is over. They take the deadly flirtation for the romantic marriage. The West perceives the Cold War to be over, and Communism to be dead; but from the Soviet side the *Cold War will accelerate and become more deadly*, especially for the political right which is being targeted as never before with the intention that it should suffer total obliteration.
>
> . . . In accordance with the main objective of Bloc strategy to change the balance in the Communists' favor, Communist diplomacy has started to reduce Western (and especially US) military potential through a number of diplomatic agreements while at the same time accelerating the Communist's program to increase their own military potential.
>
> One can also expect concealed Communist attempts to intensify their influence in the United States and thus oblige the United States to withdraw from overseas involvements.
>
> . . . The Soviet and Chinese rocket strike units and strategic bombers will make a surprise raid on Pearl Harbor [and] on the main government and military headquarters of the leading Western countries and on their missile sites. The main idea will be to knock out the primary Western sources of retaliation and to paralyze, at least for a short period, their physical ability to make a decision on retaliation.
>
> In their estimate, the Communist leaders may expect that the advantage of surprise, given that they will be in hiding in their secret government headquarters, will

provide them with the opportunity to paralyze Western governments and military authorities with a good chance of avoiding any retaliation.

Such an attack will probably be accompanied by an intensification in the activity of the Communist countries' intelligence agents designed to increase panic in the West and to operate blackouts and paralyze normal life in the capitals of the Western countries.

The Soviet strategists believe that an economic depression in the United States would provide even more favorable conditions for the execution of their strategy. In that event, the Soviets and their allies would shift to the doctrine of class struggle and try to divide the Western nations along crude class lines.

The final period of "restructuring" in the United States and Western Europe would be accompanied, not only by the physical extermination of active anti-Communists, but also by the extermination of the political, military, financial and religious elites. Blood would be spilled and political re-education camps would be introduced. The Communists would not hesitate to repeat the mass repressions of their revolution in 1917, of the Soviet occupation of Eastern Europe in the Second World War or of the Chinese Communist victory of 1949.

This time, they would resort to mass repressions in order to prevent any possibility of revolt by the defeated, and to make their victory final. . . . Their vision includes the extermination of the American and European capitalists and elites.

. . . The current joke among Soviet bureaucrats in Moscow is said to be that "*perestroika*" will be followed by "*perestrelka*"—that is to say, a "shoot-out," ending in a bloodbath in the Lenin-Stalin style.

. . . In his predictions made in 1967, [Dr. Andrei] Sakharov said that "restructuring," disarmament, socialist convergence and the creation of a World government could be complete by the year 2,000. His timetable may have slipped a bit but, given Western ignorance of Soviet strategy and the West's erroneous response to Gorbachev, the worst may happen.[5]

Golitsyn acknowledges that his vision of a surprise attack on the West is only his own speculation at this time. It is his belief, however, that it is a very real possibility, one that the KGB has researched and studied extensively. In any case, considering the accuracy of his previous record, it is one possible scenario that America should be prepared for.

As far back as 1989, CIA deputy director Robert Gates, skeptical about Soviet reforms, was warning the country of the massive Soviet arms buildup. The April 14, 1989 issue of the *Wall Street Journal* reported that Gates had stated that: "*Every report we get is that new mobile intercontinental nukes like the SS-24 & SS-25 continue to roll off the production lines, as do blackjack bombers armed with Cruise missiles, advances in anti-missile defenses & submarines.*" (emphasis added) While warning of the extraordinary scope and sweep of Soviet military modernization, and weapons research development, Gates confirmed that "at this point, we see no slackening of . . . weapons production or programs."[6]

Should the reader still have any doubts about Russia's and China's continued targeting of U.S. cities the following headline and article was printed in the *Washington Times*, in June of 1998. It should help clear up the matter:

Russia's bombers train to strike U.S., not China

Russia's strategic bomber forces recently carried out simulated nuclear bombing raids against the United States in exercises that included test firings of long-range cruise missiles, The Washington Times has learned.

According to a Defense Intelligence Agency (DIA) assessment of the exercises, the bomber activity

---

[5] Golitsyn, Anatoliy, *The Perestroika Deception: The World's Slide Towards 'The Second October Revolution'* ['WELTOKTOBER'], p. 40, 170-172, 34, 38, 63, 41.

[6] "Cold War Facts," *Wall Street Journal*, Vol. 213, No. 13, April 14, 1989, p. A14.

"demonstrated that the heavy bomber force is still an important factor in Russia's strategic planning . . .

"The April exercises indicate that the primary mission of the heavy bomber force remains strikes on North America," the DIA stated.

. . . Most of Russia's strategic bombers took part in the Long-Range Aviation exercises, which were held April 20-27 [1998] in Central Asia as part of a nationwide spring military training cycle. . . .

The large-scale exercise involved most of the Russian Air Force's long-range bombers, including Tu-95 Bear and Tu-160 Blackjack bombers, which both carry long-range nuclear cruise missiles.

. . . The Blackjack can carry up to 12 cruise missiles and the Bears each can be fitted with six AS-15s.

. . . The bombers flew simulated raids into northern polar regions—the flight path used for attacking the United States, the officials said.

. . . The simulated bomber attacks against the United States were not the first time Russian nuclear units targeted U.S. or allied forces.

During a command post exercise held in March and April of last year [1997], Russian military commanders called in nuclear strikes on a simulated attack by NATO ground forces and Lithuanian and Polish troops along the Poland-Belarus border.

. . . In addition to the continued threat from Russia's bombers, a recent CIA report said China is aiming 13 of its long-range strategic missiles with nuclear warheads at U.S. cities.[7]

The July 8, 1998 Internet edition of the *Washington Post* reported in an Associated Press article that former Soviet agent Stanislav Lunev, a former colonel in the

---

[7] Bill Gertz, "Russia's bombers train to strike U.S., not China," *The Washington Times*, National Weekly Edition, June 15-21, 1998, p. A1. Also see John Diamond, "CIA report says some Chinese missiles aimed at U.S.," The Associated Press, *Post Register*, May 3, 1998, p. F6.

Russian military intelligence service, disclosed that not only is the Russian military preparing for a future war against NATO and the United States, but they are also gathering information on the President, "key congressional and military leaders and members of the cabinet for assassination squads."[8] Lunev alerted CIA and FBI officials of the following Russian covert preparations against the U.S.:

> ". . . Russia remains terrified of the power of America, and Russian military intelligence does everything it can to prepare for a war that it considers inevitable."
>
> . . . Elite troops already are training in the United States and in the event of war "would try to assassinate as many American leaders as possible, as well as their families."
>
> . . . They would also blow up power stations, telephone switching systems and dams and target secret landing sites for Air Force One.
>
> . . . Lunev said special agents were entering the United States as foreign tourists on fake passports and that elite troops were locating sites to deposit small nuclear devices, known as "suitcase bombs," in the Shenandoah Valley outside Washington and the Hudson Valley of New York.
>
> . . . Insisting that Russia was preparing for war with the United States, the former intelligence officer said Russian pilots are training for action against NATO and the U.S. military. Russia still consider[s] the United States and NATO the main potential military adversaries.[9]

These alarming reports clearly show the hostility with which Russia and China still view the U.S. Western security will continue to be compromised unless this threat is taken seriously by our government and intelligence officials. On August 12, 1998, U.S. Rep. Floyd Spence, a 14-term Congressman and chairman of the House National

---

[8] Barry Schweid, "Defector Warns of Russian Plans," *The Washington Post*, The Associated Press, http://search.washingtonpost.com/wp-srv/WAPO/19980708/V000418-070498-idx.html, July 8, 1998.

[9] *Ibid.*

Security Committee, while speaking at a Chamber of Commerce luncheon, stunned many of his listeners when he warned them of this country's lack of military readiness.

> Everything seems to be going pretty well for all of us. But what if all of a sudden the lights went out? What if the phones wouldn't work? What if the computers wouldn't work? What if all of your automobiles wouldn't work?
>
> Think a minute about what that could do to your life . . . And that could happen if someone exploded a nuclear device hundreds of miles above the Midlands.

Spence went through similarly scary scenarios involving a terrorist releasing anthrax into the air over the area and somebody in Russia accidentally hitting a button launching a nuclear missile toward us.

> We don't have a defense against these things, and the greater problem than that is most people don't realize it.
>
> . . . Americans have been lulled into a false sense of security.

When an audience member asked Spence why people hadn't heard about the country's susceptibility to these threats, he said it was because they weren't listening.

> It's out there in the media. But people don't want to think about bad things. . . . They can't conceive of it happening. It sounds like Star Wars to them. They think it can't happen in the real world, but it can happen in this real world.[10]

To counter this growing menace of nuclear annihilation, the U.S. needs to develop a competent national anti-ballistic missile defense system. An effective ABM system would improve America's defenses and limit her vulnerability to a surprise ballistic missile attack by shooting down any incoming enemy missiles. History is replete with examples of nations who were ultimately overcome by their own false

---

[10] Joey Holleman, "Spence warns of military unreadiness," *The State*, http://www.thestate.com/daily/local/spence13.htm, August 13, 1998.

sense of security. If America continues to go unshielded from this type of danger, how long do you think it will be before one of her enemies decides to take advantage of this weak link in her defenses? Remember the proliferation of countries with nuclear capabilities is increasing, not decreasing, thus so is the danger.

Communism Needs Western Capital

In the 1992 book, *Russia's Secret Rulers: How the Government and Criminal Mafia Exercise Their Power*, by Lev Timofeyev, he explains how he obtained a Communist Party Central Committee document that was dated August 23, 1990 (a year before the communist coup in 1991). The paper provides evidence that the Communists were preparing to go underground. The leadership of the Communist Party realized that they could not modernize the nation without a massive amount of Western capital. They also realized that Western businessmen would be very unwilling to invest large sums of money into an economy as heavily indebted as theirs. To overcome this they began to speak publicly about privatization and covertly started to seize as much for themselves as possible and turn it into private property. Timofeyev stated that "long before the collapse of above-ground Communist Party structures in August, 1991, apparatchiks were carefully planning political action to preserve the maximum of power in secret Party structures."[11] Timofeyev then went on to explain how "the old Party apparatus has deeply concealed its *underground* structure."[12] Criminal prosecutors who were involved in beginning an investigation in October of 1991, "found more than a hundred commercial Communist Party enterprises in Moscow and about six hundred all told

---

[11] Lev Timofeyev, *Russia's Secret Rulers: How the Government and Criminal Mafia Exercise Their Power*, 1992, as quoted in *Youth Action News*, July, 1993, p. 5.
[12] *Ibid.*

throughout Russia. Among the direction of these shadowy Party firms are *people who have substantial influence in the current legitimate government.*"[13]

Russia feels that the West, particularly America, has been completely deceived by their overtures of peace. They feel that they have succeeded in instilling into the West a huge false sense of security, and the stage is now set for Russia and her allies to successfully launch a war when the West is least prepared and least expects it.

The Russian military has been applying an increasing amount of pressure on Boris Yeltsin to appoint political hard-liners to powerful positions within his cabinet. In the April 5, 1993 issue of *U.S. News and World Report* it was reported that: "The [Russian] General Staff has the technical ability to decide who has nuclear authority. . . . The General Staff has the technical ability to launch a nuclear-tipped missile *without Yeltsin's approval.*"[14]

In the May 5, 1997 issue of *The Spotlight,* it was noted in a top-secret report released by the CIA, that U.S. intelligence has been monitoring underground military facilities being built by Russia, Iran and North Korea. It stated that Russia was spending billions for the construction and development of mammoth nuclear safe command posts for Russian leaders. "The original intention for their construction was the view of leaders of the former Soviet Union that it could survive, with the underground bunkers, a nuclear war with the United States."[15] The CIA document also states that work is continuing on a "nuclear-survivable, strategic command post at Kosvinsky Mountain," located about 850 miles from Moscow deep

---

[13] *Ibid* (emphasis added).

[14] Bruce B. Auster, "The Armed Forces: How They Line Up", *U.S. News and World Report*, Vol. 114, No. 13, April 5, 1993, p. 52 (emphasis added).

[15] Mike Blair, "Enemies Go Underground," *The Spotlight*, Vol. 23, No. 6, May 5, 1997, p. 24.

within the Ural Mountains."[16] It has been revealed in U.S. satellite photos that work is moving ahead on another enormous facility at Yamantau Mountain also located 850 miles from Moscow in the Urals, close to the town of Beloretsk. The CIA account also suggested "that a special nuclear-proof bunker at Voronovo, some 46 miles south of Moscow is now virtually complete."[17] It also reported that there is another bunker at Harapovo, which is located 34 miles from Moscow and has a special underground railway leading to it. These anti-nuclear bunkers are being built despite the fact that they cannot afford food or housing for their people. All this underground construction *"shows they take the threat of nuclear war so seriously that they're willing to spend scarce resources on it."*[18]

The Yeltsin government is also maintaining ongoing research and development of ELF (Extremely Low Frequency) weapons for use against the West. These weapons can disrupt brain function, cause mental stress and even kill a targeted victim. It has been shown that these electromagnetic fields have a direct effect on the vertebrate nervous system.[19] These weapons can also be utilized against U.S. guidance control systems in missiles, tanks, aircraft, etc., as a series of mysterious Navy accidents indicates.[20]

Russia and Her Allies Expand Their Biological Weapons

Not only is the military in control of many of the nuclear warheads but they are also pressing forward with secret biological warfare programs. The following chilling report appeared in the July, 1993 *Youth Action News* research report by C.B. Baker:

[16] *Ibid.*
[17] *Ibid.*
[18] *Ibid.*
[19] See C.B. Baker, "Covert E.L.F. Aggression," *Youth Action News*, December, 1989, p. 3.
[20] *Ibid.*, p. 1.

The 8/31/92 *Washington Post* reported that the U.S. and Britain are worried that the Russian government may not have fulfilled a promise to shut down the Soviet Union's extensive program for making germ weapons: "Underlying U.S. concerns is the suspicion that the highly secret former Soviet program *is not yet fully under President Yeltsin's control*, and that elements of it *have been hidden by Russian military officials* who want to keep parts of the program intact. . . . A high-level Soviet defector claimed that Moscow engaged in *systematic deception* on biological warfare issues throughout the 1980's.

"The defector revealed that for the first time, Moscow had not just one, but two biological warfare programs. Besides the obviously military-run program that had provoked longstanding U.S. concern, the government was also conducting secret germ weapons research in the *civilian Biopreparat facilities*." The charge was denied by former Soviet President Gorbachev. But Russian President Yeltsin admitted to U.S. President Bush in February, 1992 that "the Soviet military had violated an international treaty, negotiated in 1972, barring development, production or stockpiling of toxin and biological agents and any weaponry to deliver them."

A confidential report, prepared in spring, 1992 at Yeltsin's direction by a retired Russian general, Anatoly Kuntsevich, revealed that the military had illicitly developed aerial bombs and rocket warheads capable of carrying deadly anthrax, tularemia and Q fever biological warfare agents. . . . Yeltsin responded to Kuntsevich's report by issuing a decree in April, 1992 ordering such work halted and its funding halted.

The Soviet defector's information "provoked anxiety about the size of the biowar program and how far (the Soviets) had gotten in producing weapons *carrying deadly viral strains that may be resistant to vaccines*."

The 2/1/93 *Newsweek Magazine* reported that the Soviet Union's biowar program involved "a vast operation employing 25,000 people at 18 or more research and development facilities, six production plants and a major storage complex in Siberia. *The goal was to take known pathogens and alter their genetic structures to make them resistant to western drugs.*" The Soviet defector, Vladimir Pasechnik, was a microbiologist who had firsthand knowledge of the enormous biowar program *aimed against the West.*[21]

It has been reported that the Soviets have also been involved in genetic engineering. In addition, there have been reports of their splicing the gene responsible for the toxic component in cobra venom into common organisms making it easy to disseminate. It has also been revealed that the Russians have developed a weapon based on the Ebola virus.[22]

Even with these potential dangers being brought to light, it would appear that many of our state public health agencies are still dangerously underinformed concerning the possibility of a chemical or biological attack. In fact, "Central Intelligence Agency Director John Deutch warned that the threat of chemical and/or biological attack in the U.S. is 'the most urgent, long-term pressing intelligence challenge we face.'"[23]

Reinforcing this feeling, Senator Sam Nunn of Georgia stated in March of 1996 that the United States had a "remarkable lack of domestic preparedness."[24] In 1996, Congress, responding to intelligence briefings concerning the biological/chemical threat to the United States, ordered the Pentagon to take the lead in preparing city and state governments to respond to the growing terrorist threat involving chemical or biological weapons. They

---

[21] C.B. Baker, "The New Russian Threat & E.L.F. Zapping," *Youth Action News*, July, 1993, p. 3 (emphasis added).
[22] See Joseph D. Douglass, Jr., "A Biological Weapons Threat Worse Than Saddam," *The Wall Street Journal*, March 10, 1998, p. A22.
[23] Steve Macko, "The Threat of Chemical and Biological Attack," *Emergency Net News*, August 27, 1996,http://www.emergency.com/chembio3.htm.
[24] *Ibid.*

devised a training program intended to help 120 of our largest cities deal with the possibility of terrorist use of nuclear, chemical and biological weapons by the end of 1999. The General Accounting Office reported that as of the middle of April, 1998, "police, firefighters and emergency medical teams in fewer than two dozen cities have completed the training."[25] It is apparent that even with this ongoing program, it will take some time to bring local emergency agencies and emergency medical personnel up to speed.

On February 25, 1998, the ABC News program Prime Time Live broadcast a program with Diane Sawyer about the dangers of Germ Warfare in today's world. Two of the main guests on this program were Ken Alibek and Dr. Michael Osterholm of the Minnesota Department of Health. Alibek is a former Soviet Biological weapons expert and first deputy chief of the Main Directorate Bioreparat. In this position Alibek was second in command over biological weapons research.

Alibek has been called the most important defector the U.S. has ever had on biological warfare. Alibek confirmed that Soviet scientists had perfected virus superstrains that no current vaccine can touch that could wipe out the entire population of Earth several times over. Alibek acknowledged "that as late as 1992, just before he left Russia, they had directly targeted American cities in the event of war for a biological first strike"[26] with plague, smallpox, and anthrax. He said that these particular weapons were chosen because they were very contagious and had a high mortality rate. They are weapons that "can cause absolute destruction of vital activity. . . . Each missile has 10 warheads. And inside are special bomblets filled with biological weapons."[27]

---

[25] *The Post Register*, April 24, 1998, p. A12.
[26] Diane Sawyer, "Germ Warfare Weapons of Terror," *Prime Time Live Transcripts*, February 25, 1998, p. 8.
[27] *Ibid.*, p. 9.

Each of the targeted cities would not have just one disease applied against them, but rather a cocktail of between three to five different biological agents. Alibek said that Russia has at least "fifty-two biological agents that would be used in their biological weapons"[28] and that it's virtually impossible to vaccinate or protect people against 52 different biological agents because nobody could survive after 52 vaccinations.

Dr. Michael Osterholm of the Minnesota Department of Health warned of the grave danger facing our communities and state agencies if they remain uninformed and unprepared for the possible threat of a biological attack:

> It is not a matter of if this will occur. It's a matter of when it occurs and where it occurs, and how much panic and how much death are we willing to accept at the time that it occurs.
>
> I can't imagine in any major city in this country, with a major release of anthrax, that there'll be ever enough antibiotics appropriate for that illness on hand when that illness first starts to show up.
>
> Probably the greatest misconception we have in this country is that we are actually really preparing ourselves as a country for a biological terrorist event.
>
> There hasn't been a single alert put out to the public health system of this country. No letters, no phone calls, no suggestions about how to coordinate the situation. [29]

Osterholm then goes on to warn that the first responders to this type of attack will not be the firemen or police. It will be uninformed and unprepared health agencies, and they won't recognize the symptoms of these unusual diseases brought on by a bioattack. Osterholm says that the health officials can become casualties themselves, and yet these individuals are going virtually untrained.

---

[28] *Ibid.*, p. 10.
[29] *Ibid.*, p. 2, 15, 20-21.

Diane Sawyer pointed out at the end of this interview that experts now believe that "the nuclear threat may have shifted and that the threat of the 21st century will be biological."[30]

In May of 1998, responding to the seriousness of this biological threat, President Clinton ordered the stockpiling of antibiotics and vaccines to treat large numbers of civilians in the event of a biological attack against the United States. He also directed the upgrading of public health and medical surveillance systems to detect any release of viruses or bacteria and sound the alarm. U.S. officials have stated that as many as ten countries now have the capability of loading anthrax spores into weapons.[31]

On April 29, 1997, in an *Associated Press* release, it was reported that with the inclusion of the United States there were currently 87 countries that had ratified the worldwide treaty banning chemical weapons. "The pact bans the use, development, production or stockpiling of all chemical warfare agents and requires that countries destroy existing stockpiles over the next decade."[32] Russia, which admits to having amassed vast reserves of these chemical agents, has yet to sign on. Russia's failure to sign the pact keeps them in full agreement with their previously stated objectives to mislead and weaken the U.S. position while strengthening theirs.

The September 24, 1992 issue of the *Washington Times* reported: "For years, the Soviets have been calling for a ban on anti-satellite weapons, arguing that space should be weapon-free." Apparently this public posture applies only to the United States, as "Russia appears to have developed

---

[30] *Ibid.*, p. 23.
[31] See Bradley Graham, "Clinton Calls for Germ War Antidotes," *Washington Post*, p. A01. Also see Terence Hunt, Associated Press, "President Clinton warns of cyberattack threat," *The Post Register*, May 23, 1998, p. A5.
[32] Associated Press, "Weapons Treaty Takes Effect Without Russia," *The Post Register*, Vol. 66, No. 154, April 29, 1997, p. A6.

two different kinds of anti-satellite weapons, while the United States has none."[33]

The January, 1998 edition of *Reader's Digest* reported that U.S., European and Israeli intelligence officials have confirmed, with the assistance of American spy satellites, that Russian engineers and technicians are giving the Iranian long-range missile program a sweeping amount of technological assistance in the development and deployment of a family of new-generation ballistic missiles. They are equipped with modern advanced-guidance systems and are based at least in part on the Soviet SS-4 strategic rockets. The CIA states that this threat goes even further to include the development of chemical, biological and nuclear weapons.

Western intelligence reports indicate that the *Shahab-3* missile is closest to deployment. It will carry 1650 pounds of explosives 800 miles—allowing Iran to hit every major city in Israel, the Persian Gulf oil fields and the bases in Saudi Arabia and Turkey where American forces are stationed. A *Shahab-3* carrying the anthrax germ could kill millions.

Currently under development is an even more powerful missile, the *Shahab-4*. It can carry a one-ton warhead 1250 miles, making it capable of devastating cities and populations in nations as far away as Egypt. Iran is also moving forward with the development of solid fuel missiles with a 2800-mile and 6300-mile strike-range. These missiles are capable of reaching targets as distant as London and Paris and cities within the eastern United States.

Intelligence sources say that this transfer of Russian missile technology is tentatively scheduled to be in production in early 1999. With the help of the Russians, Teheran is significantly extending her hostile reach throughout the world. This technological support gives Iran a decisive military edge in the Middle East and poses

---

[33] James Hackett, "Russia's Sudden ASAT," *Washington Times*, Vol. 11, No. 268, September 24, 1992, p. G1.

an enormous threat to the national security of the United States and her allies as well.[34]

According to the UN Special Commission on Iraq (UNSCOM), UN inspectors have uncovered Iraqi records that prove Iraq, as well, has an ongoing program to produce biological weapons of mass destruction. They documented a strategy to use biological and chemical warheads in an unprovoked first-strike. The report outlined some of the substances Iraq tested for possible use as biological weapons that included anthrax, clostridium prefringens (gas gangrene), which causes human flesh to rot, botulinum toxin, which results in muscular paralysis and death.[35]

The mass destructibility these germ weapons can cause was reported in the November 21, 1997 issue of the *New York Times*.

> Just a flask of culture can produce pounds of anthrax bacteria in four days. One gram—about 0.04 ounces, or the weight of two paper clips—contains enough doses to kill 10 million people.
>
> Botulinum toxin, another agent prepared by Iraq, is one of the most poisonous substances known. The lethal dose is one billionth of a gram per kilogram, meaning that breathing in 70 billionths of a gram would kill a person weighing 70 kilograms or 154 pounds. The toxin is fatal within three days to 80 percent of those exposed.
>
> But to serve as weapons, both anthrax and botulinum toxin need to be inhaled. That requires gently dispersing them as a mist at ground level, a difficult task in war conditions. . . .

---

[34] See Kenneth R. Timmerman, "Missile Threat From Iran," *Readers Digest*, January, 1998, pp. 87-91. Also see Bill Gertz, "China assists Iran, Libya with missiles," *The Washington Times*, National Weekly Edition, June 22-28, 1998, p. A1.

[35] See Joel Himelfarb/Charles Perkins, "UN: Iraqi Biological Weapons" http://www.aipac.org/hot/MiddleEast/neriraq.html, America Israel Public Affairs Committee.

Someone who efficiently distributed anthrax at a low altitude over a city could kill millions . . . A recent report by the Office of Technology Assessment described agents like anthrax as "true weapons of mass destruction with a potential for lethal mayhem that can exceed that of nuclear weapons."

Anthrax is not contagious but possesses another feature that adds to its fearsomeness: its spores, like radioactivity, can persist for decades.[36]

In the Jan/Feb, 1998 issue of *MIT's Technology Review*, Jonathan B. Tucker stated that pound for pound, biological weapons containing disease-causing microbes and natural poisons, such as anthrax, pneumonic plague and botulinum toxin, rival nuclear weapons in their ability to impose large numbers of casualties on mankind. Tucker directs the chemical and biological nonproliferation project of the Center for Nonproliferation Studies at the Monterey Institute of International Studies in Monterey, California. In 1995 he served as an inspector on a UN Special Commission team investigating biological weapons activity in Iraq, including the suspected Al Hakam facility near Baghdad.

A biological attack could create an almost unimaginable catastrophe. According to an estimate by the U.S. Congress's former Office of Technology Assessment, 100 kilograms of anthrax, released from a low-flying aircraft over a large city on a clear, calm night, could kill 1-3 million people. This figure is comparable to the casualties from a one-megaton hydrogen bomb. When disseminated as an aerosol, anthrax spores (analogous to microscopic seeds) are inhaled deep into the victim's lungs and travel to the lymph nodes, where they germinate and multiply. The bacteria then secrete potent toxins, giving rise in about three days to a devastating illness.

---

[36] Nicholas Wade, "Germ Weapons: Deadly, but Hard to Use," *New York Times*, November 21, 1997.

. . . Because biological weapons are so potent yet much cheaper and easier to produce than nuclear weapons, they have been called "the poor man's atomic bomb."

Iraq is only the best-known example of several countries—among them China, Egypt, Iran, Iraq, Libya, North Korea, Sudan, Syria and Taiwan—known or suspected to be pursuing a biological warfare capability. The U.S. government also believes that rogue elements within the Russian military may be continuing Soviet programs to develop biological weapons, despite President Boris Yeltsin's 1992 order that such activities cease.[37]

The Threat of Vladimir Zhirinovsky

Soviet/Russian analyst and author, Jay Adams, has written numerous editorials concerning the dangers of this strategic Communist deception that is now being orchestrated by Moscow. In February of 1995, he warned of the following possible scenario, which was widely distributed to the media and over the Internet:

A crucial feature of Moscow's strategy involves staging a radical power reversal in Russia so that policies of Westernization can be abruptly replaced by militant anti-Western pursuits. . . Moscow's specific plan is to bring Vladimir Zhirinovsky to power, probably through a bogus coup, prior to launching its attack.

. . . Moscow plans to shift blame for global war onto the West by underhandedly provoking the U.S. and its allies into taking military action against Russian allies-of-old. With the collapse of communism, the U.S. has taken on the role of "world policeman." This has provided Moscow an opportunity to lure the U.S. and its military allies into a trap, particularly by using the United Nations.[38]

Zhirinovsky blatantly stated in 1991 what his draconian policy would be if he should gain control of the

---

[37] Jonathan B. Tucker, "Putting Teeth in the Biological Weapons Ban," *MIT's Technology Review*, January/February 1998, pp. 38-45.

[38] Jay Adams, *A Global War?*, http://syninfo.com/J/j02.html, p. 5.

Russian presidency: "I say it quite plainly—when I come to power, there will be a dictatorship."[39] He has become one of the most formidable forces in Russian politics. It is widely believed that his political rise is due to KGB ties. Zhirinovsky's views have attracted "soldiers, police (both secret and civilian) and managers of weapons plants. He calls for more soldiers, more law enforcement, more weapons production"[40] and a return of Russia to the old Soviet borders. This man definitely bears watching.

Adams stated that Moscow may try to manipulate the U.S. by luring them into various flashpoint conflicts around the world such as the Balkans, North Korea, Iraq, Iran and other Persian Gulf hot spots.

> By luring the West into conflicts with Russian allies-of-old, Moscow creates a pretext for launching world war three. First off, a bogus Zhirinovsky coup can be thrown in Moscow, possibly along with an untimely demise of Boris Yeltsin from ill-health or death. Meanwhile, due to a "nationalist backlash" stemming from Western "imperialist aggression" against historical Russian allies like the Serbs, a pretext is created for launching world war three.[41]

The November 9, 1996 edition of the *New York Times* reported that "despite an economic boom, Russians have increasingly blamed democracy and capitalism for crime and corruption—a backlash that has fueled the appeal of nationalist figures like Vladimir Zhirinovsky and Aleksandr Lebed."[42] It matters little whether it is Yeltsin, Lebed, Zhirinovsky or another Russian leader yet to show up on the scene. The communist plan for the destruction of the USA and total world domination is still the same. The

[39] Kevin Fedarko, "A Force to Be Reckoned With," *Time*, December 27, 1993, p. 36.
[40] Victoria Pope, "A New Face of the Old Russia," *U.S. News & World Report*, December 27, 1993/January 3, 1994, p. 32.
[41] Jay Adams, *A Global War?*, http://syninfo.com/J/j02.html,pp. 13-14.
[42] Stephen Handelman, "Can Russia's Mafia Be Broken," *New York Times* (Late New York Edition) November 9, 1996, p. 23.

stage has now been set for a massive Communist attack against the West by Russia and her allies. She is continuing to prepare for this coming conflict and appears to be only waiting for the most opportune moment to strike.

Joel M. Skousen has cautioned against believing the dangerous illusion that the Soviets are presenting to the world. Skousen is the author of *Strategic Relocation: North American Guide to Safe Places*. He is also a designer of high security residences and retreats, which offer protection against natural disasters, economic collapse and nuclear war. Skousen points out in his book that there is powerful evidence indicating that preparation for a future first-strike against the United States is still the main goal of Russian Communism.

> Perhaps the biggest ruse that has ever been foisted upon an educated society is the oft repeated declaration that "COMMUNISM IS DEAD."[43]

> The so-called "collapse of the Soviet Union" is a fraud, engineered by the Soviets themselves in concert with the Sun Tzu doctrine of *"feigning weakness to cover preparations for war."* If they are no longer targeting our cities, as Clinton claims, why are they building four new underground nuclear bunkers in Moscow for the elite? Why are they spending billions on an underground nuclear weapons storage and manufacturing facility in the Ural mountains? Why are they continuing to develop new chemical and biological agents in violation of all treaties? Why did they demand in the new ABM treaty that our anti-ballistic missiles be *limited to less than 3,000 feet per second?* Why do they want us *not to build any ABMs*, and if we do, to make sure they are so slow, they can't catch missiles? The only conceivable explanation for any of these non-defensive acts is that they are planning a surgical surprise attack on our nuclear military forces, in the future. President Clinton [announced on December 10,

---

[43] Joel M. Skousen, *Strategic Relocation: North American Guide to Safe Places*, 1998, p. 132.

1997] that he is directing the US military to change their nuclear doctrine—first, we are no longer to prepare to win a nuclear war, only deter it. And second, he announced to the world that the US *will not launch on warning*, and that missile silos will *no longer be on alert status*. But the second announcement precludes any deterrence. The only real deterrence to a Russian strike (which takes about 20 minutes to arrive on target) *is to launch on warning*—so that our silos are empty when hit and their military targets suffer major damage in the return strike. Now, with no alert status, it guarantees that we couldn't even change our minds in time to launch, even if we wanted to. *This suicidal strategy actually invites a first strike*— and the bigger the better for Russia (or even China someday), since they have nothing to lose.[44]

The bottom line is that *we are headed for the worst war in the history of the world*. It will come, I believe, in the *first decade of the next century*, when our disarmament is at a maximum and their buildup is nearly complete. The US has agreed to dismantle its Minute Man II Missiles (though they aren't being destroyed yet). The US has agreed to decommission the 50 peacekeeper MX missiles—our only land-based missiles capable of penetrating Russian hardened targets. It has agreed to stop keeping nuclear armed B-52s on alert. It has removed the nuclear capabilities of the B-1 bomber and the entire Naval Fleet. It has agreed to not build anymore Trident Submarine bases except those in Bangor, Washington and Kings Bay, Georgia.

. . . It is my general feeling that the Russians have a certain window of opportunity to strike in the future. This window is defined by the maximum disarmament they can get the West to achieve, and maximum strength they can build secretly. When these two aspects reach the highest point of advantage for the Russians, they will strike.

[44] Joel M. Skousen, Advertising flyer for his book *Strategic Relocation: North American Guide to Safe Places*, 1998.

. . . The Russians are really worried about ballistic missile defenses since their entire strategy is built upon a massive first strike.

. . . It is doubtful that we will ever really see an operational anti-ballistic missile defense system (ABM). But if it does get close to deployment, the Russians will surely strike before it becomes operational. Furthermore, the longer the Russians wait, the more obvious their deceptions become and the more their refusals to disarm illuminate their future intent to strike.[45]

Skousen further believes that Russia will have an ideal window of opportunity for a surprise attack on the U.S. sometime in the first decade of the next century due to America's present disarmament policies, probably somewhere around 2003-2008. With all the implications that indicate Russia as a possible future antagonist against America, it is this author's opinion that the real question we should be asking ourselves is not *if* Russia will attack the United States, but *when*.

Many of the previous dreams and visions discussed in this book depict a surprise third world war being initialized against America by Russia. The sweeping devastation that will result from this attack will be used by the Lord as an instrument to punish a sinful nation and to prepare, cleanse and refresh America for her future glory. The Lord is going to "chasten his people with many afflictions . . . with death and with terror, and with famine and with all manner of pestilence . . ." (Helaman 12:3) There will be such a scene of pain, suffering, bloodshed and death throughout this land that the more righteous of the survivors will wish that their memory of these grim days would fail them. The reports of calamity, carnage and inhuman ravages throughout this land will fill the eyes of the Saints with tears. The hearts of men everywhere will be filled with dread, despair and defeat. ". . . The wicked shall slay the

---

[45] *Op. Cit., Strategic Relocation*, pp. 138-139.

wicked, and fear shall come upon every man; And the
Saints also shall hardly escape; nevertheless, I the Lord,
am with them, and will come down in heaven from the
presence of my father and consume the wicked with
unquenchable fire." (D & C 63:33-34)

Heber C. Kimball has confirmed that it was revealed to
him that during this time of bloodshed, fire and thunder,
the last great destruction of the wicked in America would
be on the lakes near the Hill Cumorah.[46] Notice the similarities between this future prophecy of the judgments that
are to come upon America and the final struggles of the
Jaredite and Nephite nations. (see Ether 14:22, Omni 1:22,
Mormon 6:15) In all cases the severity of the judgments left
the unburied dead scattered all across the face of the land.

This extensive depopulation of the earth will set the
stage for a righteous remnant to form the nucleus or foundation from which a purified millennial population will
emanate.

---

[46] N.B. Lundwall, *Inspired Prophetic Warnings*, pp. 51-52.

Consequences of War Devastating

I n a Conference address, President Benson described what the aftermath of war and bombing in World War II was like:

> People [were] half-starved, with all their earthly belongings on their backs.
>
> . . . I remember, my brethren and sisters, great tracts of once fertile and productive land lying idle. The anomaly of land idle, and people starving because there was no seed to plant, no machinery with which to plant, cultivate, and harvest, and no power because power machines had been destroyed and horses had been killed during the bombings and many others killed and eaten for human food!
>
> . . . the aftermath of the war is usually worse than the actual physical combat. Everywhere there is the suffering of old people, innocent women and children. Economies are broken down, the spirits of people crushed, men and women bewildered and a spirit of frustration prevails. It is a saddening thing to see people who have lost their freedom—the right to choose—who have lost their right to move about freely, to assemble together as we meet here today. I recalled, too, the sin and corruption, the immorality and the starvation that always follow war.[1]

Aftermath of an Atomic Attack

As the horrifying realization of what has happened begins to set in, the survivors of a nuclear attack will become painfully aware of the unique problems they will need to overcome. Unique in that America has never been

---

[1] Ezra Taft Benson, *Conference Report*, October, 1952, pp. 118-119.

attacked by a foreign power on our soil in the 48 contiguous states in the 200-plus years since the American Revolution. It will come as a total shock to the American people, and the majority of them will be taken completely off guard.

The enormous amount of energy that will be unleashed by an atomic attack will undoubtedly loose the forces of nature in all her destructive fury. Massive earthquakes and volcanic eruptions will follow, creating great fissures in the earth and spewing ash and other contaminants into the already darkened heavens. The atmosphere will become even darker from the fire, smoke and fumes caused by the great atomic explosions.

Millions will be destroyed by these blasts, and many more will die from exposure to radiation. Fires will rage out of control, with no one left to fight them, adding to the already dangerous levels of air pollution that cover the face of the land. Underwater volcanoes will create new land masses, and great earthquakes will take place in the world's oceans causing gigantic tidal waves to roar in and engulf some of the remaining major coastal cities.

There will be a lack of sanitary facilities and because of this, infectious diseases will spread more swiftly than before. There will be relatively few medical institutions left intact for the sick and injured who have survived the catastrophe. Those who have knowledge of herbs and the natural healing arts will undoubtedly be in great demand. Many will perish from a weakened immune system due to lack of food and exposure to the elements. Food, water and shelter will become the most precious of commodities to the remaining population, and all those left, both the righteous and unrighteous, out of necessity, will have to band together in order to survive.

More than likely, this type of unexpected attack will bring a complete breakdown of all forms of existing government, and criminal gangs will immediately step in and fill the void. Riots, vandalism and anarchy will become the order of the day in the major cities that are left throughout the country. The great diversity of races and religions that make up America today will fragment into smaller ethnic-based groups. Open warfare will emerge between these groups as the lack of vital necessities worsens. Communications and electrical power sources will have been destroyed, and mechanized transportation will be completely shut down. Without the distribution of food and the other basics of life that normally move continuously across our country via trucking and rail, we will be in great danger of famine.

These great catastrophic events that are coming upon the American continent in the near future necessitate the study of the words of the Lord concerning this time period and the adequate preparation of the Saints, both spiritually and materially, for these events if they want to survive them.

The Lord has not left us without warning. We have received sufficient warnings concerning this future period of time. The scriptures as well as our church leaders have testified that these things must surely come. The spirit of the Lord is descending upon many people throughout this country and upon others, warning of the impending warfare and destruction that is going to come upon this nation and the world. The Lord does not warn his children of these things unless he wants them to prepare and take some sort of anticipatory action to survive this coming holocaust. There are many other similar dreams/visions that also could have been used in this book; however, those that have been shared paint a clear picture and warning that unless America repents as a nation, she will be attacked and laid waste.

We have been told for centuries that a great destructive force was going to be turned loose on the earth. Ancient and modern prophets who have seen it in vision have vividly described it as an "abomination of desolation" (see Matthew 24:15; Joseph Smith-Matthew 1:12, 32). Only in our generation have we come to realize how literally these prophecies can be accomplished through the scientific advancements in *thermonuclear reaction*, the precursor to a devastating *thermonuclear war*.

How many of the Saints will be prepared for the coming devastation, desolation and sifting that will accompany this attack on our nation, and how many will be lulled into a false sense of security, believing that this type of scenario could never happen here? You decide which category you fit in. The choice and the responsibility are yours. We have been warned.

What Can the Saints Do to Prepare?

In the Welfare Conference of October 11, 1958, President J. Reuben Clark, Jr. spoke of his anxiety concerning a great war that he felt was yet to come. Because there have been many modern technological advancements since his talk was first given, his statements have become even more applicable to us today.

> I still have apprehension that we may have hard times. I still fear that we are going to have a war before too long that on each side will be intended to be a virtually exterminating war. I would like each one of you to think of having around you—you farmers—production that would enable you to live (*and possibly for a while without too much mechanization*), and help some of your city folk to live, too. It is a terrible picture even to think about, *but we will be shortsighted if we do not.*[2]

In the September 1961, issue of the *Improvement Era* President Clark again stated his belief that America would one day be engulfed in atomic warfare.

> We heard him reply in answer to a question as to why he had put his life savings into his presently owned Grantsville ranch; "This is all I have to leave to my family when I die, and if they are not too lazy to work it, they

---

[2] J. Reuben Clark, Jr., Welfare Conference, The Assembly Hall, October 11, 1958 (emphasis added).

won't starve. I have told them that when the first atomic bomb is dropped here in America, that they are to go out there on the ranch and stay until it is over." *This last* [statement] *seemed not only to be wise council, but also a prophecy.*[3]

We can also rest assured that America will never experience this type of attack until as a nation we have forsaken the God of this land. "We need not fear invasions from without, so long as we as a nation and as a people understand and uphold the Constitution of the United States, and reject not the God of the land who is Jesus Christ. But if we permit ourselves to forget God, we have no promise."[4]

If we ever completely turn from the fundamental principles of Christianity and constitutional government, we will then be in danger of losing many of our freedoms, for the Lord has decreed that whosoever should possess this land must worship Him or be swept off (see Ether 2:10).

President Benson admonished the Saints to be faithful to the laws of God and serve him and they would prosper in the land for "no nation which has kept the commandments of God has ever perished, but I say to you that once freedom is lost, *only blood—human blood— will win it back.*[5]

Food Storage:
A Necessary Preparation for Survival

In the June,1982 issue of the *Ensign*, F. Enzio Busche, a member of the First Quorum of the Seventy and a survivor of the devastation and total destruction in Germany during World War II, gave the following suggestions for

---

[3] Harold B. Lee, "President J. Reuben Clark, Jr.—An Appreciation on His 90th Birthday," *Improvement Era*, Vol. 64, No. 9, September, 1961, pp. 632-633 (emphasis added).

[4] ElRay L. Christiansen, *Conference Report*, October, 1967, p. 139.

[5] Ezra Taft Benson, "A Witness and a Warning," *Ensign*, Vol. 9, No. 11, November, 1979, p. 33 (emphasis added).

necessities and other storage items that he found were the most needed:

> As for what we needed, the food item we relied on most was vegetable oil. With a bottle of vegetable oil, one could acquire nearly every other desirable item. It had such value that with a quart of vegetable oil one could probably trade for three bushels of apples or three hundred pounds of potatoes. Vegetable oil has a high calorie content, is easy to transport, and in cooking can give a tasty flavor to all kinds of food items that one would not normally consider—wild flowers, wild plants, and roots from shrubs and trees. For me and my family, a high-quality vegetable oil has the highest priority in our food storage, both in times of daily use and for emergency usage. When vegetable oil is well-packed and stored appropriately, it has a long storage life without the necessity of refrigeration. We found ours to be in very good condition after twenty years of storage, but circumstances may vary in different countries and with different supplies.
>
> . . . The second highest priority item for *me and my family* is grain in all its forms, preferably wheat and rye. When grain is well-packed and well-preserved, it too is easy to transport, easy to store, and will last for generations.
>
> A third priority item is honey. Its value in daily usage is immeasurable. My family prefers honey rather than sugar because our experience supports some of the research findings regarding the preeminence of honey. Another reason I prefer honey is because during the starvation period in postwar Germany, honey could be traded for three times as much as sugar; its value was considered that much greater.
>
> A fourth important food storage product is powdered milk.
>
> These four basic items—oil, wheat, honey, and milk (*or their equivalents in other cultures*)—together with water, salt, and renewable basic foods such as potatoes, and other vegetables, can satisfy nutritional requirements in

times of emergency and also are valuable and usable in normal daily life.

You might ask, "What about the many other food items and desserts that play an important role in our eating habits?" I shall always treasure the great experience I had in those hard times, when I learned to appreciate food with the most balanced nutrients. *When a person is very hungry, the taste of food will change for him. In times of emergency, the Lord seems to provide a way to help our bodies adapt.*

. . . When we think in terms of our own year's supply of those foods and materials we use on a regular basis, we may feel that every family will have to store everything. This, of course, is not easy and seems to make storage difficult. However, let me offer this comforting idea based on past experience. We need to take into consideration that in difficult times, so long as there survives more than one family, there will be trading of valuable items. A free market will begin immediately to satisfy the needs of people, and items in greatest demand will set the price, bypassing the use of money. The ingeniousness of mankind becomes evident in times of need. When man is presented with a problem or challenge, if he is in a healthy spirit—which hopefully we are—he will find solutions that he never dreamed of. When a person has a good, healthy spirit, is able to adjust and is not afraid to use his imagination, he will find ways to survive.

There is a long way from the point of hunger to actual starvation, and there is much that one can do to stay alive in hard times, especially when one is mentally and physically prepared. A garden even as small as a window box, is of great value, as is the skill to be able to plant and to grow things. Following the war, in addition to having a small garden, my family was able to obtain the milk we needed by keeping a milk sheep, which gave enough milk for our family for the greater part of the year. (I have not seen this species in America, but it was very common in Germany.) Besides milk, our sheep supplied us with wool to trade or to use for knitting items. During the spring of the year it would give birth to one or two lambs which could also be used for food or trade. . . . Also, all over the country, even the large cities, people began to keep rabbits in small pens, and children had the task of looking for grass, dandelions, and leaves in order to feed their rabbits. In addition, people kept hens, and chicken coops were prevalent in all places. Because grain was too valuable to feed to chickens, other sources of chicken feed had to be found. Children found ways of breeding worms, beetles, and flies to be used for this purpose. People also built small, wooden handcarts which could be used to transport items used for trading, which took place wherever people met.

. . . The true nature of people becomes obvious in times of real need. Good people become better; they get close to one another; they learn to share and become united. The strength that develops out of unity of the many good people becomes a real survival factor. On the other hand, people who lack emotional stability become cruel and ruthless under trying circumstances; however, they do not seem to become an overbearing threat because of the closeness and unity of the majority of the people. Therefore, strangely enough, those who have survived hardships look back with fond memories to the awful period of pain and destruction because they recall the closeness that developed as they united themselves by sharing whatever they had.[6]

Grains, garden seeds, water, water purification tablets, powdered milk, honey, soap (*for hands, dishes and clothing*), toilet paper and cold weather clothing should be among the first necessities that you acquire for your storage program. You can always expand your storage items after you have obtained the most essential basics.

The Lord tells us that he has "decreed wars upon the face of the earth" (D&C 63:33), that there will be "famines,

---

[6] F. Enzio Busche, "How Beautiful to Live in These Times and Be Prepared," *Ensign*, Vol. 12, No. 6, June, 1982, pp. 16-19 (emphasis added).

and pestilences, and earthquakes" (Matthew 24:7), and that mankind will be afflicted by "an overflowing scourge; for a desolating sickness shall cover the land" (D&C 45:31).

We are warned that the elements will be in great commotion with famine and plague, thunder and lightning, and great earthquakes (See D&C 87:6). "The waves of the sea shall heave themselves beyond their bounds" (D&C 88:90), and the earth itself will "reel to and fro as a drunken man" (D&C 49:23).

It seems that there will come a time when there will be many different judgments sent to annihilate the harvest of the field. In Doctrine and Covenants 29:16 we are told that "there shall be a great hailstorm sent forth to destroy the crops of the earth." This will happen "because of the wickedness of the world," and the Lord will "take vengeance upon the wicked" (D&C 29:17) and He will use famine and pestilence to call the people unto repentance. Can there be any doubt that there will be other calamities that shall occur as well?

President Ezra Taft Benson has noted that "these particular prophecies seem not to be conditional."[7] Yet through all of these calamities the Lord has said, *"if ye are prepared ye shall not fear"* (D&C 38:30, emphasis added). We have been warned for over 100 years to be prepared, to store up grain and other emergency foodstuffs so that we may survive these critical times when they come upon us.

When will all these calamities strike? We do not know the exact time, but it appears it may be in the not-too-distant future. Those who are prepared now have the continuing blessings of early obedience, and they are ready. Noah built his Ark before the flood came, and he and his family survived. Those who waited to act until after the flood began were too late."[8]

---

[7] Ezra Taft Benson, "Prepare Ye," *Ensign*, Vol. 4, No. 1, January, 1973, p. 81.

[8] *Ibid.*

President Ezra Taft Benson has spoken often of the re
ponsibility we have to set our temporal house in order, that
we may not be classed among the foolish and unprepared:

> *We have a duty to survive, not only spiritually but phys-*
> *ically.* . . . for we face days ahead which will test the moral
> and physical sinews of all of us.
>   . . . *A man should not only be prepared to protect him-*
> *self physically, but he should have on hand sufficient sup-*
> *plies to sustain himself and his family in an emergency.*[9]

It is our obligation and duty to prepare for future uncer-
tainty by initiating an adequate food storage program for
our families, along with other life-sustaining essentials for
future periods of instability and upheaval, as the brethren
have counseled.

In Salt Lake City, at General Conference on October 5,
1856, President Brigham Young addressed the importance
of the Saints attending to their temporal duties while calling upon them to send relief supplies of food and other
necessities to the stranded Willie Handcart Company. His
advice is still pertinent today.

> I will tell you all that your faith, religion, and profession
> of religion, will never save one soul of you in the Celestial
> Kingdom of our God, unless you carry out just such prin-
> ciples as I am now teaching you. . . . *Attend strictly to those*
> *things which we call temporal, or temporal duties. Other-*
> *wise, your faith will be in vain. The preaching you have*
> *heard will be in vain to you, and you will sink to Hell,*
> *unless you attend to the things we tell you.*[10]

These statements lend credence to the scripture in
James 2:20: "faith without works is dead." In the April
Conference of 1965, President Benson once again voiced a

---

[9] Ezra Taft Benson, *An Enemy Hath Done This*, pp. 59, 60 (emphasis
     added).

[10] Brigham Young, *Journal of Discourses*, Vol. 4, p. 113. Also see LeRoy
     R. Hafen, and Ann W. Hafen, *Handcarts to Zion 1856-1860*, p. 121
     (emphasis added).

similar warning to the membership of the church. "Should the Lord decide at this time to cleanse the Church . . . a famine in this land of one year's duration could wipe out a large percentage of slothful members, including some ward and stake officers. *Yet we cannot say we have not been warned.*"[11]

Our church leaders have admonished the saints many times over to prepare for difficult times. Where possible, fruit trees, grapevines, berry bushes, vegetables and other similar items should be planted. You should also obtain a year's supply of garden seeds for planting the following year. We have been asked to become proficient in the sewing and mending of our own clothing.[12] Are we following the counsel that has been given, or have we been deceived into believing we can keep postponing it until tomorrow?

Many in the church now have grown to adulthood never knowing about the effects that calamity, depression, hunger, homelessness and joblessness can bring upon a nation. Many others think that some form of assistance will always be available from some government or church crisis center if an emergency does arise. To those of you who find yourself in this foolish and complacent category, President Spencer W. Kimball has given the following caution:

> The great difficulty is that when difficult times come those who in normal times could lend assistance are also under the wheel of the grinding mill. It may be impossible to anticipate and prepare for the eventualities of *depression, war, invasion, bombing,* but we can go a long way.[13]

---

[11] Ezra Taft Benson, "Not Commanded in All Things," *The Improvement Era*, June, 1965, pp. 537-539 (emphasis added).

[12] See Vaughn J. Featherstone, "Food Storage," *Ensign*, Vol. 6, No. 5, May, 1976, pp. 116-118. Also Spencer W. Kimball, "Family Preparedness," *Ensign*, Vol. 6, No. 5, May, 1976, pp. 124-126.

[13] Spencer W. Kimball, *The Teachings of Spencer W. Kimball*, p. 372 (emphasis added).

The Lord has given us revelation warning of the difficult days that lie ahead. We are now in the day when many of you living will see the fulfillment of those prophecies. Great tribulations await this generation because of its wickedness. Truly we live in the generation of which the Savior spoke, when "the love of men shall wax cold, and iniquity shall abound." (D&C 45:27) It is only in our day that this wickedness will become so well organized and rampant throughout America and the world that the world will be cleansed by fire.

It is our responsibility to heed the counsel of our leaders and prepare for the worst while the sun still shines and the crops still grow. Let's hope we do not find ourselves in the same position as those who laughed and jeered while Noah was building the ark, only to find out later that the rain was indeed beginning to pour down. Concerning this type of attitude Elder Mark E. Petersen warned:

> There are many very good people who keep most of the Lord's commandments with respect to the virtuous side of life, but who overlook His commandments in temporal things. They do not heed His warning to prepare for a possible future emergency, apparently feeling that in the midst of all this trouble "*it won't happen to us.*"
>
> . . . To prepare for the future is part of God's eternal plan, both spiritually and temporally. To protect ourselves against reversals and hardships is only good sense.[14]

And President Brigham Young gave these words of warning:

> If you are without bread, how much wisdom can you boast, and of what real utility are your talents, *if you cannot procure for yourselves and save against a day of scarcity those substances designed to sustain your natural lives?*

---

[14] Mark E. Petersen, "Blessings in Self Reliance," *Ensign*, Vol. 11, No. 5, May, 1981, p. 62 (emphasis added).

. . . If you cannot provide for your natural lives, how can you expect to have wisdom to obtain eternal lives?[15]

We must follow the Lord's admonition to the Saints of this dispensation: "Prepare yourselves for the great day of the Lord." (D&C 133:10)

President Ezra Taft Benson has confirmed that "this preparation must consist of more than just casual membership in the Church. We must be guided by personal revelation and the counsel of the living prophet so we will not be deceived."[16]

As a not-too-distant future that is filled with calamities and judgments of God draws ever closer, we can be confident. If we do all in our power to prepare ourselves for whatever perils lie ahead, the Lord will bless us with whatever else we may require, because of our early obedience. Out of the most catastrophic destruction and upheaval ever to be manifest upon mankind, an era of righteousness will be born. Prosperity and a restoration and regeneration of the earth that has never before been experienced, will come about.

[15] Brigham Young, *Journal of Discourses*, Vol. 8, p. 68.

We believe in the literal gathering of Israel and in the restoration of the Ten Tribes; that Zion (the New Jerusalem) will be built upon the American continent; that Christ will reign personally upon the earth; and, that the earth will be renewed and receive its paradisiacal glory.

—10th Article of Faith

The Age of Restoration

efore moving on, it is necessary that we review and make sure that we have a correct understanding of the meaning of the term "restoration of all things." (D&C 27:6; 86:10) It implies that something that was once possessed, is lost, and that it will eventually be replaced or restored to its original condition. From the scriptures we learn that the earth was first created in a paradisiacal or Edenic state. (see 2 Nephi 2:19-25; Genesis 2; 3; Moses 3; 4) It was a terrestrial abode for all life until the fall of man, when it underwent a change and became a telestial sphere. The ground of the earth then became cursed and brought forth thorns and thistles to afflict man. (see Genesis 3:17-18) Until that time all life was immortal, as death had not entered the world and all things were still in the perfect state in which they were created. (2 Nephi 2:19-25)

The restoration started in the spring of 1820 with the appearance of the Father and the Son to the Prophet Joseph Smith. This was the beginning of "the times of restitution" (Acts 3:21) to which Peter referred.

With all the doom and gloom in the world, the teachings of the prophet Joseph Smith pierce through the veil of darkness and despair that accompany the wicked and unenlightened, to lift the righteous of the world to a true knowledge of God's plan. The prophet has said that this is a great period of time. The righteous of all ages have looked forward to this generation with great delight and gladness. It is an end result in which all the honest, virtuous and upright will take great pleasure, anticipation and joy, as

the powers of Satan are overcome and the kingdom of the
Lord bears rule.

The building up of Zion is a cause that has interested
the people of God in every age; it is a theme upon which
prophets, priests and kings have dwelt with peculiar
delight; they have looked forward with joyful anticipation
to the day in which we live; and fired with heavenly and
joyful anticipations they have sung and written and
prophesied of this our day; but they died without the
sight; we are the favored people that God has made
choice of to bring about the Latter-day glory; it is left for
us to see, participate in and help to roll forward the Latter-day glory, "the dispensation of the fullness of times,"
when God will gather together all things that are in heav-
en, and all things that are upon the earth, "even in one,"
when the Saints of God will be gathered in one from every
nation, and kindred, and people, and tongue, when the
Jews will be gathered together into one, the wicked will
also be gathered together to be destroyed, as spoken of by
the prophets; the Spirit of God will also dwell with His
people, and be withdrawn from the rest of the nations,
and all things whether in heaven or on earth will be in
one, even in Christ. The heavenly Priesthood will unite
with the earthly, to bring about those great purposes;
and whilst we are thus united in the one common cause,
to roll forth the kingdom of God, the heavenly Priesthood
are not idle spectators, the Spirit of God will be showered
down from above, and it will dwell in our midst. The
blessings of the Most High will rest upon our tabernacles,
and our name will be handed down to future ages; our
children will rise up and call us blessed; and generations
yet unborn will dwell with peculiar delight upon the
scenes that we have passed through, the privations that
we have endured; the untiring zeal that we have manifested; the all but insurmountable difficulties that we
have overcome in laying the foundation of a work that
brought about the glory and blessing which they will realize; a work that God and angels have contemplated with

delight for generations past; that fired the souls of the ancient patriarchs and prophets; a work that is destined to bring about the destruction of the powers of darkness, the renovation of the earth, the glory of God, and the salvation of the human family.[1]

The Earth to Receive Its Paradisiacal Glory

"The restoration will include resurrection, regeneration, and renewal to all life upon the earth and the glorification of the earth itself, when it becomes a celestial sphere." (Isaiah 65:17; Matthew 19:28; Revelation 21:1; D&C 29:22-25; 88:17-20, 25-26)[2]

Isaiah 65:17-25 and Doctrine and Covenants 101:23-31 speak of a time when everything will be changed, when the earth will pass from its "telestial" state to its "terrestrial" or paradisiacal state. This is comparable to the type of existence that was before the fall. This great renewal and "transfiguration" (D&C 63:20-21) of the earth will be so remarkable and sweeping that the former conditions "shall not be remembered, nor come into mind." (Isaiah 65:17)

Joseph Fielding Smith has cautioned that many Saints misunderstand what the true condition of the earth will be at this time of renewal:

> We are living in the great day of restoration. The Lord has declared that all things are to be restored to their primitive condition. Our Tenth Article of Faith says, "We believe . . . that Christ will reign personally upon the earth; and, that the earth will be renewed and receive its paradisiacal glory." Too many have the idea that this has reference to the celestialized earth, but this is not the case. It refers to the restored earth as it will be when Christ comes to reign.[3]

---

[1] Joseph Smith, *History of the Church*, Vol. 4, pp. 609-610.
[2] Cory H. Maxwell, "Restoration of All Things," *Encyclopedia of Mormonism*, Vol. 3, pp. 218-219.
[3] Bruce R. McConkie, Compiler, *Doctrines of Salvation: Sermons and Writings of Joseph Fielding Smith*, Vol. 1, p. 84.

This will be a day of great destructive change, when the earth will be broken down, dissolved and moved exceedingly to and fro like a drunkard, the whole world will be in commotion. (Isaiah 4:19-20) So great and terrible will be the destruction that *"the saints that are upon the earth, who are alive, shall be quickened and be caught up"* (D&C 88:96, emphasis added) *by the Lord in order to be saved from the devastation.*

Peter spoke of this day as "the times of refreshing." (Acts 3:19) There will be "a great earthquake, such as was not since men were upon the earth;" (Revelation 16:18) a day when the continents themselves will begin to change and move until they again unite into one grand landmass. "The great deep shall roll back into the north countries and . . . the land of Zion and the land of Jerusalem shall be joined together"[4] and "the earth shall be like as it was" in the days of Peleg, "in the days before it was divided." (D&C 133:24, Genesis 10:25) The mountains and valleys will no longer be found. (D&C 133:22)

All these changes in the earth "shall cause groanings in the midst of her, and men shall fall upon the ground and shall not be able to stand." (D&C 88:89) All of this is but the "preparation by which the earth and its inhabitants will approach foreordained perfection. The final stages of this regeneration of nature will not be reached until the Millennium has run its blessed course."[5]

Concerning the final state of the earth, the *Encyclopedia of Mormonism* has this to say:

> "We believe . . . that the earth will be renewed and receive its paradisiacal glory." (Articles of Faith 10) LDS revelation declares that the earth is destined to become a celestial body fit for the abode of the most exalted or celestial beings. (D&C 88:8-20, 25-26) This is a unique departure from the traditional Christian beliefs that heaven is

---

[4] William Phelps, "The Last Days," *Evening and Morning Star*, Vol. 1, No. 9, February, 1833, p. 65.

[5] James E. Talmage, *Articles of Faith*, p. 375.

the dwelling place for all saved beings, and that after fulfilling its useful role the earth will become uninhabited, or be destroyed. Doctrine and Covenants 130:9 teaches that finally the earth will become sanctified and immortalized, and be made crystal-like. The "sea of glass" spoken of in Revelation 4:6 "is the earth, in its sanctified, immortal, and eternal state." (D&C 77:1)[6]

This latter-day regeneration, refreshing and restitution will return the earth to its former paradisiacal glory and terrestrial state which will be brought to pass by the Second Coming of the Savior preparatory to His glorious Millennial reign. The ultimate destiny of the earth is of course to become a celestial sphere, a fit abode for angels and gods to reside.

---

[6] Morris S. Petersen, "Earth: The Origin and Destiny of the Earth," *Encyclopedia of Mormonism*, Vol. 2, p. 432.

This earth, in its sanctified and immortal state, will be made like unto crystal and will be a Urim and Thummim to the inhabitants who dwell thereon, whereby all things pertaining to an inferior kingdom, or all kingdoms of a lower order, will be manifest to those who dwell on it; and this earth will be Christ's.

—D & C 130:9

15

A Celestial City
for a Celestial Planet

In Revelation 20:2-3, we learn that after the closing of the Millennial reign, Satan, who was bound, shall be loosed a little season and he "shall go out to deceive the nations which are in the four quarters of the earth" (Revelation 20:8) again. He will be so successful in his deception of mankind at this time that he will be able to gather together a great army of the wicked, and so numerous will be their numbers that Satan will be able to surround "the beloved city . . . the camp of the saints" (Rev. 20:9) with his legions. Michael will then return and "gather together his armies, even the hosts of heaven" (D&C 88:112). He will call fire down from God out of heaven, and devour them, and they shall be cast "into the lake of fire and brimstone" where they "shall be tormented day and night for ever and ever" (Rev. 20:9-10). Then, will come the end of the paradisiacal or terrestrial earth and it will need to be purified, die and receive its resurrection.

The City of Zion, or the New Jerusalem, will then be taken from the earth until it is cleansed and prepared for its celestial glory. Then, when the earth has been sufficiently prepared for celestial life and celestial glory, the city will come down a second time, to a purified celestial planet, that has become like unto a "sea of glass and fire" or a Urim and Thummim. Those that dwell upon it will be able to know all things that they desire whether past, present or future by gazing into it (D&C 130:7; 77:1).

The prophet Joseph Smith taught that the Gods live in "everlasting burnings" and that the righteous saints who have lived on the earth "shall rise again to dwell in everlasting burnings in immortal glory, not to sorrow, suffer, or die any more, but they shall be heirs of God and joint heirs with Jesus Christ."[1]

President Joseph Fielding Smith also taught that this earth is a living entity that must be baptized, die, be resurrected, and ultimately celestialized.[2] After the earth is sanctified and celestialized, this earth will become the home of the "Church of the Firstborn," and the presence of the Father and the Son in the New Jerusalem [will] take the place of the temple, for the whole city, due to their presence, would become a temple.[3] The earth will then become an everlasting residence for the righteous of this world that shines like the sun, as the following scripture explains:

> And the end shall come, and the heaven and the earth shall be consumed and pass away, and there shall be a new heaven and a new earth.
>
> For all old things shall pass away, and all things shall become new, even the heaven and the earth, and all the fulness thereof, both men and beasts, the fowls of the air, and the fishes of the sea;
>
> And not one hair, neither mote, shall be lost, for it is the workmanship of mine hand. (D&C 29:23-25)

The celestial city will be so magnificent that it defies mortal description. However, we do have a hint of what it will be like in John's vision of the beloved city, "the holy Jerusalem" recorded in Revelation 21:11-27:

> Having the glory of God: and her light *was* like unto a stone most precious, even like a jasper stone, clear as crystal;

---

[1] Joseph Fielding Smith, *Teachings of the Prophet Joseph Smith*, pp. 372, 347.

[2] Bruce R. McConkie, Compiler, *Doctrines of Salvation: Sermons and Writings of Joseph Fielding Smith*, Vol. 1, pp. 87-88, 73.

[3] Bruce R. McConkie, Compiler, *Doctrines of Salvation: Sermons and Writings of Joseph Fielding Smith*, Vol. 2, p. 244.

And had a wall great and high, *and* had twelve gates, and at the gates twelve angels, and names written thereon, which are *the names* of the twelve tribes of the children of Israel:

On the east three gates; on the north three gates; on the south three gates; and on the west three gates.

And the wall of the city had twelve foundations, and in them the names of the twelve apostles of the Lamb.

And he that talked with me had a golden reed to measure the city, and the gates thereof, and the wall thereof.

And the city lieth foursquare, and the length is as large as the breadth: and he measured the city with the reed, twelve thousand furlongs. The length and the breadth and the height of it are equal.

And he measured the wall thereof, an hundred *and* forty *and* four cubits, *according to* the measure of a man, that is, of the angel.

And the building of the wall of it was *of* jasper: and the city *was* pure gold, like unto clear glass.

And the foundations of the wall of the city *were* garnished with all manner of precious stones. The first foundation *was* jasper; the second, sapphire; the third, a chalcedony; the fourth, an emerald;

The fifth, sardonyx; the sixth, sardius; the seventh, chrysolite; the eighth, beryl; the ninth, a topaz; the tenth, a chrysoprasus; the eleventh, a jacinth; the twelfth, an amethyst.

And the twelve gates *were* twelve pearls; every several gate was of one pearl: and the street of the city *was* pure gold, as it were transparent glass.

And I saw no temple therein: for the Lord God Almighty and the Lamb are the temple of it.

And the city had no need of the sun, neither of the moon, to shine in it: for the glory of God did lighten it, and the Lamb *is* the light thereof.

And the nations of them which are saved shall walk in the light of it: and the kings of the earth do bring their glory and honour into it.

And the gates of it shall not be shut at all by day: for there shall be no night there.

And they shall bring the glory and honour of the nations into it.

And there shall in no wise enter into it any thing that defileth, neither *whatsoever* worketh abomination, or *maketh* a lie: but they which are written in the Lamb's book of life.

The prophet Joseph Smith in vision saw that it was Father Adam who stood by and opened the gate of the Celestial City to the righteous. He would then conduct them to the throne of God, one by one, where they were embraced by the Savior and crowned Kings and Priests forever.[4]

President David O. McKay shared the following account of a celestial vision he received describing the city and its inhabitants:

I . . . beheld in a vision something infinitely sublime. In the distance I beheld a beautiful white city. Though far away, yet I seemed to realize that trees with luscious fruit, shrubbery with gorgeously tinted leaves, and flowers in perfect bloom abounded everywhere. The clear sky above seemed to reflect these beautiful shades of color. I then saw a great concourse of people approaching the city. Each one wore a white flowing robe, and a white headdress. Instantly my attention seemed centered upon their Leader, and though I could see only the profile of his features and his body, I recognized him at once as my Savior! The tint and radiance of his countenance were glorious to behold! There was a peace about him which seemed sublime—it was divine!

The city, I understood, was his. It was the City Eternal; and the people following him were to abide there in peace and eternal happiness.

But who were they?

---

[4] See Heber C. Kimball, *Journal of Discourses*, Vol. 9, p. 41.

As if the Savior read my thoughts, he answered by pointing to a semicircle that then appeared above them, and on which were written in gold the words:

"These Are They Who Have Overcome The World—Who Have Truly Been Born Again!"[5]

The Lord has said that there will be very few who will qualify for the blessing of eternal life. He explains that "Strait is the gate, and narrow is the way, which leadeth unto life, and few there be that find it." (Matthew 7:14) There will be many Latter-day Saints who will not gain the celestial glory which could have been theirs because they did not abide the commandments of God. Those who are not entitled to receive a fullness of this greater glory and its blessings will be assigned to a lower kingdom attended to by those who have received it; the higher kingdoms to minister to the lower.[6]

Could the Kingdom of Glory that we ultimately attain be contingent upon our efforts to preserve, maintain and perpetuate the principles of freedom brought forth in America and bequeathed to us by the power of God in the divinely inspired Constitution? It seems so. In General Conference, October, 1950 a Prophet and President of the Church, David O. McKay, gave this solemn warning to the membership:

No greater immediate responsibility rests upon members of the Church, upon all citizens of this Republic and of neighboring Republics *than to protect the freedom vouchsafed by the Constitution of the United States.*[7]

Those, then, who are members of the church, who have received more light, and who are not obedient to

---

[5] *Cherished Experiences*, p. 102, as cited in L.G. Otten & C.M. Caldwell, *Sacred Truths of the Doctrine and Covenants*, Vol. 2, pp. 390-391.

[6] See Bruce R. McConkie, Compiler, *Doctrines of Salvation: Sermons and Writings of Joseph Fielding Smith*, Vol. 2, pp. 244 5-6.

[7] David O. McKay, *Conference Report*, April, 1950, p. 37.

this directive, and do not fulfill this great responsibility, duty and calling from the Prophet, may be jeopardizing their own future exaltation in the Celestial Kingdom.

Special Requirements Placed Upon the Land of Promise

Hugh Nibley aptly describes the special requirements that the Lord places on those whom he allows to settle in this hallowed land of promise:

> God does not bring people to the promised land for a repeat of the Old World follies; here he is determined to "raise up unto me a righteous branch from the fruit of the loins of Joseph. Wherefore, I the Lord God will not suffer that this people shall do like unto them of old." (Jacob 2:25-26) God's people may never enjoy the luxury of living after the manner of the world. (see D&C 105:3-5) The promised land is a testing ground offering both great opportunity and corresponding risk: "Wherefore, this people shall keep my commandments, saith the Lord of Hosts, or cursed be the land for their sakes." (Jacob 2:29) In the Old World are civilizations which were ancient at the time Lehi left Jerusalem, and they still survive, but of those in the land of promise we are told that when they are ripe in iniquity, when the cup is full, they shall be swept off from the land. Compared with other continents, this one has no history, no surviving cultures, though far and wide civilizations whose identities remain a mystery have left their ruins and their scattered descendants.[8]

President Hugh B. Brown gave the following counsel concerning the attitude which the saints should have towards America and the perpetuation of our freedoms:

> We inherited the choicest land of all the earth and with it the freedom vouchsafed by an inspired Constitution. Freedom cannot be static or passive, it must be active,

---

[8] Hugh Nibley, *Collected Works of Hugh Nibley: The Prophetic Book of Mormon*, Vol. 8, p. 478.

nurtured, and maintained. Always remember that you hold this heritage in trust for those who, in turn, will come into possession and management upon your exit from the stage. Do not betray your trust.

Become aware of and partake of the glory which is America. Your Americanism should be a "cry in the heart, a fire in the brain, a prayer in the soul" as it was defined recently by a happy refugee. The following appraisal is from *Sunshine Magazine.*

God built a continent with glory and filled it with treasures untold. He bedecked it with soft, rolling prairies, and pillared it with thundering mountains. He studded it with sweetly flowing streams and mighty winding rivers. He graced it with deep shadowed forests, and filled them with song. But these treasures would have meant little if the myriads of people, the bravest of the races, had not come, each bearing a gift and a hope. They had the glow of adventure in their eyes, the glory of hope in their souls, and out of them was fashioned a nation, blessed with a purpose sublime. They called it America. Yes, this is America, yet in these troublesome times it is well to remember what Daniel Webster said: "God grants liberty only to those who live it and are always ready to guard and defend it. Let our object be our country. And, by the blessing of God, may that country become a vast and splendid monument, not of oppression and terror, but of wisdom, of peace, and of liberty, upon which the world may gaze with admiration forever!"[9]

Exaltation and continuation of the family unit is the goal we should all be striving for. However, we will only achieve this objective if we properly prepare for the coming trials and tests that the Lord has for us in mortality. Our obedience to the Lord's commandments will be the deciding factor. It's all dependent on us.

---

[9] Hugh B. Brown, *The Abundant Life,* p. 48.

Bibliography

"1492 Voyage Fulfilled Prophecy," *Church News*. Salt Lake City, Utah: Deseret News Press. September 26, 1992.

Adams, Jay, *A Global War?* 16-page editorial widely distributed to the media and through the Internet. March 1, 1995.

Associated Press. "Weapons Treaty Takes Effect Without Russia," *The Post Register*, Volume 66, Number 154. Idaho Falls, Idaho: The Post Register. April 29, 1997.

Auster, Bruce B. "The Armed Forces: How They Line Up," *U. S. News and World Report*, Volume 114, Number 13. April 5, 1993.

Backman, Milton V. Jr. "Preparing the Way: The Rise of Religious Freedom in New England," *Ensign*, Volume 19, Number 1. Salt Lake City, Utah: Corporation of the President of The Church of Jesus Christ of Latter-day Saints. January 1989.

Baird, Amy E., Jackson, Victory H., and Wassell, Laura L., Compilers. *Mosiah Lyman Hancock (1834-1907) Autobiography (1834-1865)*. n.p.: n.d.

Baker, C.B., "Covert E.L.F. Aggression," *Youth Action News*, Alexandria, Virginia: Youth Action. December, 1989.

Baker, C.B. "The New Russian Threat & E.L.F. Zapping," *Youth Action News*. Alexandria, Virginia: Youth Action. July, 1993.

Balmforth, David N. *New Age Menace: The Secret War Against the Followers of Christ*. Bountiful, Utah: Horizon Publishers. March, 1996.

Benson, Ezra Taft. "A Witness and a Warning," *Ensign*, Volume 9, Number 11. Salt Lake City, Utah: Corporation of the President of The Church of Jesus Christ of Latter-day Saints. November, 1979.

Benson, Ezra Taft. *An Enemy Hath Done This*. Salt Lake City, Utah: Parliament Publishers. 1969.

Benson, Ezra Taft. *Conference Report*. Salt Lake City, Utah: Corporation of the President of The Church of Jesus Christ of Latter-day Saints. October, 1952.

Benson, Ezra Taft. *Conference Report*. Salt Lake City, Utah: Corporation of the President of The Church of Jesus Christ of Latter-day Saints. April, 1962.

Benson, Ezra Taft. *God, Family Country: Our Three Great Loyalties*. Salt Lake City, Utah: Deseret Book Company, 1975.

Benson, Ezra Taft. "Not Commanded in All Things," *The Improvement Era*, Volume 68, Number 6. Salt Lake City, Utah: Corporation of the

President of The Church of Jesus Christ of Latter-day Saints. June, 1965.

Benson, Ezra Taft. "Prepare Ye," *Ensign*, Volume 4, Number 1. Salt Lake City, Utah: Corporation of the President of The Church of Jesus Christ of Latter-day Saints. January, 1974.

Benson, Ezra Taft. *The Teachings of Ezra Taft Benson*. Salt Lake City, Utah: Bookcraft. 1994.

Blair, Mike. "Enemies Go Underground," *The Spotlight*, Volume 23, Number 6. Washington D.C.: Liberty Lobby, Inc. May 5, 1997.

Book of Mormon: Another Testament Of Jesus Christ, The. Salt Lake City, Utah: The Church of Jesus Christ of Latter-day Saints. 1982.

Bradford, William. *History of Plymouth Plantation 1620-1647*, Volume 1. New York, New York: Russell & Russell. 1968.

Bradshaw, Wesley. "Washington's Vision," *The National Tribune*, Volume 4, Number 12. Washington, D.C.: The National Tribune. December, 1880.

Brown, Hugh B. *The Abundant Life*. Salt Lake City, Utah: Bookcraft. 1965.

Busche, F. Enzio. "How Beautiful to Live in These Times and Be Prepared," *Ensign*, Volume 12, Number 6. Salt Lake City, Utah: Corporation of the President of The Church of Jesus Christ of Latter-day Saints. June, 1982.

Cannon, George Q. *Journal of Discourses*, Volume 14. Salt Lake City, Utah. 1967. Photo Lithographic Reprint of Exact Original Edition. Liverpool, England. 1872.

Cannon, George Q. *Journal of Discourses*, Volume 23. Salt Lake City, Utah. 1967. Photo Lithographic Reprint of Exact Original Edition. Liverpool, England. 1883.

Chittum, Thomas W. *Civil War Two: The Coming Breakup of America*. Show Low, Arizona: American Eagle Publications, Inc. 1996.

Christiansen, El Ray L. *Conference Report*. Salt Lake City, Utah: Corporation of the President of The Church of Jesus Christ of Latter-day Saints. October, 1967.

Clark, J. Reuben, Jr. *Welfare Conference*. Salt Lake City, Utah: Corporation of the President of The Church of Jesus Christ of Latter-day Saints. October 11, 1958.

"Cold War Facts," *The Wall Street Journal*, Volume 213, Number 73. Princeton, New Jersey: Dow Jones & Company, Inc. April 14, 1989.

"Columbus, Pioneers 'Courageous,'" *Church News*. Salt Lake City, Utah: Deseret News Press. July 25, 1992.

Cooperman, Alan. "There Will Be a New Union," *U.S. News and World Report*. Washington, D.C.: October 9, 1995.

Cowley, Matthias F. *Wilford Woodruff: History of His Life and Labors*. Salt Lake City Utah: Bookcraft. 1964.

Crowther, Duane S. *Inspired Prophetic Warnings*. Bountiful, Utah: Horizon Publishers. 1987.

Crowther, Duane S. *Prophecy—Key to the Future*. Salt Lake City, Utah: Bookcraft. 1962; Bountiful, Utah: Horizon Publishers, 1997.

Davidson, Lee. "Lebed Says Criticizing LDS a Mistake," *Deseret News*. Salt Lake City, Utah: Deseret News Press. March 20, 1998.

Diamond, John/Associated Press. "CIA report says some Chinese missiles aimed at U.S.," *Post Register*. Volume 67, Number 183. Idaho Falls, Idaho: Post Register. May 3, 1998.

Douglass Jr., Joseph D. "A Biological Weapons Threat Worse Than Saddam," *The Wall Street Journal*. March 10, 1998.

Dyer, Alvin R. *The Meaning of Truth*. Salt Lake City, Utah: Deseret Book Company. 1970.

Evans, Charles D. *The Contributor*, Volume 15. Salt Lake City, Utah: Young Men's Mutual Improvement Associations of the Church of Jesus Christ of Latter-day Saints. August, 1894.

Foundation for Ancient Research and Mormon Studies. *FARMS Review of Books*, Volume 8, Number 1, 1996. Provo, Utah: FARMS. 1996.

Featherstone, Vaughn J. "Food Storage," *Ensign*, Volume 6, Number 5. Salt Lake City, Utah: Corporation of the President of The Church of Jesus Christ of Latter-day Saints. May, 1976.

Fedarko, Kevin. "A Force to Be Reckoned With," *Time Magazine*, Volume 142, Number 27. New York. December 27, 1993.

Garr, Arnold K. *Christopher Columbus: A Latter-day Saint Perspective*. Provo, Utah: Religious Studies Center, Brigham Young University. 1992.

Gertz, Bill. "Russia's bombers train to strike U.S., not China" *The Washington Times*, National Weekly Edition. Washington, D.C.: News World Communications, Inc. June 15-21, 1998.

Golitsyn, Anatoliy. *New Lies for Old—The Communist Strategy of Deception and Disinformation*. New York, New York: Dodd, Mead and Company. 1984.

Golitsyn, Anatoliy. *The Perestroika Deception—The world's slide towards The 'Second October Revolution'* ['Weltoktober']. New York, New York: Edward Harle Limited. Second Edition, 1998.

Gorbachev, Mikhail. "The Gloss of Glasnost 1990," *League of Prayer*, Volume 1189. Montgomery, Alabama: League of Prayer. November, 1989.

Graham, Bradley. "Clinton Calls for Germ War Antidotes." *The Washington Post*. May 21, 1998.

Gruver, Henry. *"Russian Invasion of America,"* Virtue International. (Video tape presentation) 1825 South Franklin, Indianapolis, Indiana.

Hackett, James. "Russia's Sudden ASAT," *The Washington Times*, Volume 11, Number 268. Washington, D.C.: *The Washington Times*. September 24, 1992.

Hafen, LeRoy R. and Hafen, Ann W. *Handcarts to Zion*. Glendale, California: The Arthur H. Clark Company. 1969.

Hancock, Mosiah Lyman. *The Mosiah Hancock Journal*. n.p.: n.d.

Handelman, Stephen. "Can Russia's Mafia Be Broken?" *New York Times (Late New York Edition)*. Volume 146, Number 50606. November 9, 1996.

Himelfarb, Joel and Perkins, Charles. *UN: Iraqi Biological Weapons*. America Israel Public Affairs Committee. http://www.aipac.org/hot/MiddleEast/neriraq.html.

Holleman, Joey. "Spence warns of military unreadiness," *The State*. Columbia, South Carolina: August 13, 1998.

Horne, David Hughes. *A Vision of George Albert Smith*. Unpublished Manuscript. February 28, 1989.

Hyde, Orson. *Journal of Discourses*, Volume 6. Salt Lake City, Utah. 1967. Photo Lithographic Reprint of Exact Original Edition. Liverpool, England. 1859.

Kimball, Edward L., Editor. *The Teachings of Spencer W. Kimball*. Salt Lake City, Utah: Bookcraft. 1982.

Kimball, Heber C. *Journal of Discourses*, Volume 5. Salt Lake City, Utah. 1967. Photo Lithographic Reprint of Exact Original Edition. Liverpool, England. 1858.

Kimball, Heber C. *Journal of Discourses*, Volume 9. Salt Lake City, Utah. 1967. Photo Lithographic Reprint of Exact Original Edition. Liverpool, England. 1862.

Kimball, Spencer W. *Conference Report*. Salt Lake City, Utah: Corporation of the President of The Church of Jesus Christ of Latter-day Saints. October, 1959.

Kimball, Spencer W. "Family Preparedness," *Ensign*, Volume 6, Number 5. Salt Lake City, Utah: Corporation of the President of The Church of Jesus Christ of Latter-day Saints. May, 1976.

Kranz, Patricia. "What's Bringing Moscow Together: Fear of Lebed," *Business Week*. February 10, 1997.

"Lawmakers: U.S. must decide who's in charge of anti-terrorism." *The Post Register*. Volume 67, Number 175. April 24, 1998.

Lee, Harold B. "President J. Reuben Clark, Jr.—An Appreciation on His 90th Birthday," *Improvement Era*, Volume 64, Number 9. Salt Lake City, Utah: Corporation of the President of The Church of Jesus Christ of Latter-day Saints. September, 1961.

London Sunday Times. London: Times Newspapers, Ltd. March, 1994.

Lundwall, N. B., Compiler. *Inspired Prophetic Warnings*. Salt Lake City, Utah: Publishers Press. August, 1940.

Macko, Steve, editor. "The Threat of Chemical and Biological Attack . . ." *Emergency Net News*. August 27, 1996. http://www.emergency.com/chembio3.htm.

Manuilski, Dimitri Z. as quoted in "Deceiving America: Communist Influence in the Media." http://www.inforamp.net/~jwhitley /kgb.htm.

Maxwell, Cory H. "Restoration of All Things," *Encyclopedia of Mormonism*, Volume 3. New York: Macmillan Publishing Company. 1992.

McConkie, Bruce R. "Divers Angels," *Ensign*, Volume 10 Number 4. Salt Lake City, Utah: Corporation of the President of The Church of Jesus Christ of Latter-day Saints. April 1980.

McConkie, Bruce R., Compiler. *Doctrines of Salvation: Sermons and Writings of Joseph Fielding Smith*, Volume 1. Salt Lake City, Utah: Bookcraft. 1973.

McConkie, Bruce R., Compiler. *Doctrines of Salvation: Sermons and Writings of Joseph Fielding Smith*, Volume 2. Salt Lake City, Utah: Bookcraft. 1985.

McConkie, Bruce R., Compiler. *Doctrines of Salvation: Sermons and Writings of Joseph Fielding Smith*, Volume 3. Salt Lake City, Utah: Bookcraft. 1956.

McConkie, Bruce R. *Mormon Doctrine*. Salt Lake City, Utah: Bookcraft. 1967.

McKay, David O. *Conference Report*. Salt Lake City, Utah: Corporation of the President of The Church of Jesus Christ of Latter-day Saints. April, 1950.

McKay, David O. "Statement on Communism," *The Improvement Era*, Volume 69, Number 6. Salt Lake City, Utah: Corporation of the President of The Church of Jesus Christ of Latter-day Saints. June, 1966.

Millet, Robert L. & McConkie, Joseph Fielding. *Our Destiny: The Call and Election of the House of Israel*. Salt Lake City, Utah: Bookcraft. 1993.

Newquist, Jerreld L., Editor. *Gospel Truth: Discourses and Writings of President George Q. Cannon*, Volume 2. Salt Lake City, Utah: Deseret Book Company. 1974.

Nibley, Hugh. *Collected Works of Hugh Nibley: The Prophetic Book of Mormon*, Volume 8. Salt Lake City, Utah: Deseret Book Company. 1989.

Nibley, Hugh. *Collected Works of Hugh Nibley: Approaching Zion*, Volume 9. Salt Lake City, Utah: Deseret Book Company. 1989.

Otten, L. G. and Caldwell, C. M. *Sacred Truths of the Doctrine and Covenants*, Volume 2. LEMB, Inc. 1982.

Petersen, Mark E. "Blessings in Self-Reliance," *Ensign*, Volume 11, Number 5. Salt Lake City, Utah: Corporation of the President of The Church of Jesus Christ of Latter-day Saints. May, 1981.

Petersen, Mark E. *The Great Prologue*. Salt Lake City, Utah: Deseret Book Company. 1975.

Petersen, Morris S. "Earth: The Origin and Destiny of the Earth," *Encyclopedia of Mormonism*. Volume 2. New York: Macmillan Publishing Company, 1992.

Phelps, William, Editor. "The Last Days" *The Evening and Morning Star*, Volume 1, Number 9. Independence, Missouri: W. W. Phelps & Co. February, 1833.

Pierce, Norman C. *The Great White Chief, Echa Tah Echa Nah, The Mighty and Wise One*. U.S.A. April 6, 1971.

Pope, Victoria. "A New Face of the Old Russia," *U.S. News and World Report*. Washington, D.C.: U.S. December 27, 1993/January 3, 1994.

Pratt, Orson. *Journal of Discourses*, Volume 15. Salt Lake City, Utah. 1967. Photo Lithographic Reprint of Exact Original Edition. Liverpool, England. 1873.

Pratt, Orson. *Journal of Discourses*, Volume 18. Salt Lake City, Utah. 1967. Photo Lithographic Reprint of Exact Original Edition. Liverpool, England. 1877.

Pratt, Orson. *Journal of Discourses*, Volume 20. Salt Lake City, Utah. 1967. Photo Lithographic Reprint of Exact Original Edition. Liverpool, England. 1880.

Romney, Marion G. *Conference Report*. Salt Lake City, Utah: Corporation of the President of The Church of Jesus Christ of Latter-day Saints. April, 1968.

Ryan, Vincent. "You'll Pay for Gorbachev's Economic and Political Moves," *Spotlight*. Washington, D.C.: Liberty Lobby. May 21, 1990.

Sawyer, Diane. "Germ Warfare: Weapons of Terror," *Prime Time Live Transcripts*. http://www.abcnews.com/onair/ptl/html_files/transcripts/pt10225.html. February 25, 1998.

Schwied, Barry. "Defector Warns of Russian Plans," *The Washington Post*. The Associated Press. http://search.washingtonpost.com/wp-srv/WAPO/19980708/v000418-idx.html. July 8, 1998.

Skousen, Joel M. *Announcement for Strategic Relocation: North American Guide to Safe Places*. n.p.: n.d.

Skousen, Joel M. *Strategic Relocation: North American Guide to Safe Places*. Utah. 1998.

Skousen, W. Cleon. *The Five Thousand Year Leap*. Salt Lake City, Utah: The Freeman Institute. 1981.

Skousen, W. Cleon. *Isaiah Speaks to Modern Times*. Salt Lake City, Utah: Ensign Publishing. 1985.

Skousen, W. Cleon. *The Majesty of God's Law*. Salt Lake City, Utah: Ensign Publishing. 1996.

Skousen, W. Cleon. *Prophecy and Modern Times*. Riverton, Utah: Ensign Publishing Company. 1988.

Smith, Brian L. "I Have a Question," *Ensign*, Volume 24, Number 10. Salt Lake City, Utah: Corporation of the President of The Church of Jesus Christ of Latter-day Saints. October, 1994.

Smith, George Albert. *Conference Report*. Salt Lake City, Utah: Corporation of the President of The Church of Jesus Christ of Latter-day Saints. April, 1950.

Smith, Joseph, Jr. *History of the Church*, Volume 3. Salt Lake City, Utah: Deseret Book Company. 1973.

Smith, Joseph, Jr. *History of the Church*, Volume 4. Salt Lake City, Utah: Deseret Book Company. 1973.

Smith, Joseph, Jr. *History of the Church*, Volume 5. Salt Lake City, Utah: Deseret Book Company. 1973.

Smith, Joseph, Jr. *History of the Church*, Volume 6. Salt Lake City, Utah: Deseret Book Company. 1971.

Smith, Joseph F. *Gospel Doctrine*. Salt Lake City, Utah: Deseret Book Company. 1978.

Smith, Joseph Fielding. *The Signs of the Times*. Salt Lake City, Utah: Deseret News Press. 1952.

Smith, Joseph Fielding, Compiler. *Teachings of the Prophet Joseph Smith*. Salt Lake City, Utah: Deseret Book Company. 1976.

Smith, Joseph Fielding. *The Way to Perfection*. Salt Lake City, Utah: Deseret Book Company. 1984.

Smith, Robert W. and Smith, Elizabeth A., Compilers. *The Last Days*. Salt Lake City, Utah: Pyramid Press. 1945.

Snow, Erastus. *Journal of Discourses*, Volume 23. Salt Lake City, Utah. 1967. Photo Lithographic Reprint of Exact Original Edition. Liverpool, England. 1883.

Specter, Michael. "The Wars of Aleksandr Ivanovich Lebed," *The New York Times Magazine*, Volume 146, Number 50579. October 13, 1996.

Staker, Susan, Editor. *Waiting for World's End: The Diaries of Wilford Woodruff*. Salt Lake City, Utah: Signature Books. 1993.

Stewart, D. Michael. "I Have a Question," *Ensign*, Volume 6, Number 6. Salt Lake City, Utah: Corporation of the President of The Church of Jesus Christ of Latter-day Saints. June, 1976.

Swanson, Richard. *Spare Your People!* South Plainfield, New Jersey: Bridge Publishing, Inc. 1986.

Talmage, James E. *Articles of Faith*. Salt Lake City, Utah: Deseret Book Company. 1984.

Taylor, Charles R. *World War III and the Destiny of America.* Nashville, Tennessee: Sceptre Books. 1979.

Taylor, John. *Journal of Discourses*, Volume 21. Salt Lake City, Utah. 1967. Photo Lithographic Reprint of Exact Original Edition. Liverpool, England. 1881.

Timofeyev, Lev. *Russia's Secret Rulers: How the Government and Criminal Mafia Exercise Their Power.* Knopf. 1992.

Timmerman, Kenneth R. "Missile Threat From Iran," *Readers Digest*, Volume 152, Number 909. Pleasantville, New York: Readers Digest. January, 1998.

Tucker, Jonathan B. "Putting Teeth in the Biological Weapons Ban," *MIT's Technology Review.* South Burlington, Vermont: Lane Press. January/February 1998.

Wade, Nicholas. "Germ Weapons: Deadly, But Hard to Use," *New York Times.* New York: New York Times. November 21, 1997.

Waller, Michael. "Russia's Poisonous Secret," *Readers Digest*, Volume 145, Number 870. Pleasantville, New York: Readers Digest. October, 1994.

Wardle, Lynn D. "Seeing the Constitution as Covenant," *Ensign*, Volume 19, Number 9. Salt Lake City, Utah: Corporation of the President of The Church of Jesus Christ of Latter-day Saints. September, 1989.

Wassermann, Jacob. *Columbus, Don Quixote of the Seas.* Boston, Massachusetts: Little, Brown, and Co. 1930.

Wells, Kenneth D. "Inner Man and Outer Space," Law Day, *BYU Speeches of the Year.* Provo: Utah: Brigham Young University Press. April 30, 1962.

Woodruff, Wilford. *Journal of Discourses*, Volume 21. Salt Lake City, Utah. 1967. Photo Lithographic Reprint of Exact Original Edition. Liverpool, England. 1881.

Woodruff, Wilford. *Journal of Discourses*, Volume 22. Salt Lake City, Utah. 1967. Photo Lithographic Reprint of Exact Original Edition. Liverpool, England. 1882.

Woodruff, Wilford. *Journal of Discourses*, Volume 23. Salt Lake City, Utah. 1967. Photo Lithographic Reprint of Exact Original Edition. Liverpool, England. 1883.

Young, Brigham. *Journal of Discourses*, Volume 2. Salt Lake City, Utah. 1967. Photo Lithographic Reprint of Exact Original Edition. Liverpool, England. 1855.

Young, Brigham. *Journal of Discourses*, Volume 4. Salt Lake City, Utah. 1967. Photo Lithographic Reprint of Exact Original Edition. Liverpool, England. 1857.

Young, Brigham. *Journal of Discourses*, Volume 6. Salt Lake City, Utah. 1967. Photo Lithographic Reprint of Exact Original Edition. Liverpool, England. 1859.

Young, Brigham. *Journal of Discourses*, Volume 7. Salt Lake City, Utah. 1967. Photo Lithographic Reprint of Exact Original Edition. Liverpool, England. 1860.

Young, Brigham. *Journal of Discourses*, Volume 8. Salt Lake City, Utah. 1967. Photo Lithographic Reprint of Exact Original Edition. Liverpool, England. 1861.

Young, Brigham. *Journal of Discourses*, Volume 9. Salt Lake City, Utah. 1967. Photo Lithographic Reprint of Exact Original Edition. Liverpool, England. 1862.

Young, Levi Edgar. *Conference Report*. Salt Lake City, Utah: Corporation of the President of The Church of Jesus Christ of Latter-day Saints. April, 1960.

Index

A

B

C

H

I

J

Y

Z